THE MESSAGE OF EZEKIEL

THE MESSAGE OF
EZEKIEL
A COSMIC DRAMA

By J. TODD FERRIER

VOL. I
OF
THE LOGIA OF ISRAEL

First Published 1931
Reprinted 1988

ISBN 0 900235 10 1

Printed in Great Britain by
Redwood Burn Limited, Trowbridge, Wiltshire.

DEDICATION

To the Beloved

ROBERT

(Robert Howell Perks, M.D., F.R.C.S. ENG.)

Whose Love for the Message was sublime

and

whose Devotion to the Work was perfect

From his

Friend

I

PITY   COMPASSION   LOVE

SELF-ABANDONMENT

SELF-SACRIFICE

SELF-DENIAL

REDEMPTION

REGENERATION

ILLUMINATION

The Order of the Cross

SPIRITUAL
AIMS AND IDEALS

THE Order is an informal Brother-
hood and Fellowship, having for its
service in life the cultivation of the Spirit
of Love towards all Souls: Helping the
weak and defending the defenceless and
oppressed; Abstaining from hurting the
creatures, eschewing bloodshed and
flesh eating, and living upon the pure
foods so abundantly provided by nature;
Walking in the Mystic Way of Life,
whose Path leads to the realization of
the Christhood; And sending forth the
Mystic teachings unto all who may be
able to receive them — those sacred
interpretations of the Soul, the
Christhood, and the Divine Love and
Wisdom, for which the Order of the
Cross stands.

SERVICE   DEVOTION   PURITY

CONTENTS

THE MESSAGE OF EZEKIEL
A COSMIC DRAMA

*

PART ONE

*

THE LOGIA OF THE PROPHET'S
MESSAGE

PREFACE

The Text in this volume is a presentation of the real Message of the Prophet who bore the name of Ezekiel. It is, therefore, not to be regarded as a new translation from the MSS. obtainable which profess to contain the Message given by the Prophet. In none of the translations by the most gifted of Scholars, is there any clear conception of the Divine Purpose in the Prophet's Message, or that the Message had more than a racial and national application to the Jews. Indeed the profoundest parts of the Message are quite obscure.

The Logia of the Prophet as herein presented, were recovered by the Writer. In as far as it was possible, the terms made use of in the Book as found in the Old Testament, have been retained. In the original Message, many great Truths were revealed to the Elders of Israel which, through the redactors and translators not understanding the Masonic use of the Signs and Symbols, are quite veiled in the various MSS. and translations.

Though it may seem to the reader a great claim for anyone to make in these days, to have recovered the Message given by an Illumined One who taught the Children of Israel before Plato gave his philosophy to the Greeks, yet the Writer would have the reader understand that he makes no personal claim whatever:

3

what is claimed by him concerns the Message alone—
that it is from the Divine World whence the Prophet's
Message can alone find the true interpretation.

As in the recovery of the Days of the Manifestation as
set forth in "The Master: His Life and Teachings," and
"The Logia or Sayings of the Master," by the same
Writer, the Revelations are of no man, though the
Writer has been appointed to communicate them.

The explanation of the Text will be found in the ad-
dresses on the subject-matter of the Book which were
given to a Fellowship of Friends of the Master, and in
the Notes with Text which form the VIII Part of this
volume.

J. Todd Ferrier.

THE LOGIA
OF THE PROPHET
EZEKIEL

The hand of the Lord was laid upon me, and He upbore me to the land of Israel in the days when they were God's Ancients. There He set me down upon a very high mountain on the South side.

The mountain was as a city encompassed by walls, and within its inner walls (embrasure) stood the Temple.

When the Spirit bore me within the Temple, One, in the fashion of a man, stood before me.

His appearance was radiant as brass burnished and reflecting the glory of the Sun.

In his hand he held a line which was as of flax, and also a rod as if to measure the Temple.

He spake unto me, saying:—

'Son of Man, behold with thy vision, hear with open ear, and let thine heart be fully set upon all that is to be unveiled to thee.

Unto this end hast thou been brought hither that thou mightest declare unto the House of Israel those things which are to be shewn unto thee.'

In the days when I was a dweller in the land of the Chaldeans, the Word of the Lord came unto me.

Then were the Heavens opened, and in Vision was God revealed unto me.

As I looked into the Heavens, I beheld a Spiral Cloud whose motion was like a whirlwind with an enfolding Flame.

It was enveloped in Radiance which proceeded from out the midst of the Flame, and was like pure Amber in its colour.

From out of the Spiral there emanated the Four Living Ones.

These had the countenance of Adonai when He appears as the Divine Man.

Each of these had four Faces and six Wings.

Their feet were as standards of burnished brass, and reflected the Glory of the Radiance of the Flame.

Their Hands were like those of a Man, and they placed them under their Wings.

Their Wings were united to each other; for their powers were in unity, and moved together wheresoever they went.

The likeness of the four Faces of each of the Living Ones was that of a Man as they stood upright; on the right side the face of a Lion; on the left side the face of an Ox; and beneath they had the appearance of an Eagle.

Two of their Wings stretched upwards, and two covered their body.

In their motion they went forward; whithersoever the Spirit directed they proceeded.

And in their motion there seemed to be the appearance of four Lamps whose Flame was as a living Fire moving up and down within the Spiral of the Living Ones; and from out the Flame there emanated great radiations as when it lightneth.

And the motion of the Living Ones was such that they went forward and returned with the rapidity of a flash of lightning.

Now, as I looked upon the Four Living Ones, behold there appeared a Wheel that was fourfold.

The original Fashion of the Planet

The Wheels were the colour of Beryl, and were contained within each other, like wheels in the middle of wheels.

When they moved they proceeded upon their four sides, and they turned not in their motion.

Their centres were as exalted rings, and their spokes were full of eyes.

When the Living Ones proceeded, the Wheels went with them; when the Living Ones moved above the Earth, the Wheels were likewise lifted up.

And whithersoever the Spirit gave direction, they had their motion, for the Spirit in them responded; and the Wheels went with the living Ones; for the same Mystery that was in the Four Living Ones, was in the Wheels.

I also beheld that the Firmament stood above and rested upon the Heads of the Living Ones; the Firmament was like a great Crystal on Fire.

The Wings of the Living Ones were stretched out under the Firmament.

And when they proceeded the noise of the motion of their Wings was as the meeting of Great Waters, and as the Voice of the Omnipotent One when He speaketh to the Hosts of the Heavens.

When the Living Ones stood still, they let down their Wings.

And from out the Firmament the Voice spake to them as they stood with Folded Wings.

7

Above the Firmament that was over their Heads, I beheld a Throne come into my Vision.

It was in appearance like a great Sapphire.

And upon the Throne and yet above it, I beheld the One Who was in the likeness of the Divine Man.

He was enveloped in a Flame of Sacred Fire whose colour was like pure Amber.

The Sacred Fire moved from His Loins upward, and from His Loins downward; and as it moved it clothed Him with Resplendence.

And the Radiance was as the Rainbow round about the Throne; and it became a Cloud of Glory. For the Rainbow was the Glory of the Elohim.

When I beheld this, I bowed my Being before Him; and then did I hear the Voice of the Presence speaking to me.

And He said unto me, 'Son of Man, stand upon thy feet, and I will speak with thee.'

And I felt the motion of His Spirit within me as He raised me up to stand upon my feet, so that I was able to hearken unto what He spake unto me.

And He said, 'Son of Man, behold! I set thee as a Watchman over the House of Israel.

Therefore hear ye My Word, and proclaim it unto the House of Israel.'

Then I beheld a Roll written within and without. The Writings bore the signs of grief, sorrow and anguish; and these were concerned with the House of Israel.

And the Voice commanded me to eat the Roll. Unto me as I ate it, it was even as Honey; but soon it became bitterness unto me.

And He also said unto me, 'Son of Man, receive now into thy Heart all of My Word that I shall speak to thee, and hold the things in thy remembrance.'

A Vista of the Divine Passion

And His Spirit held me up within the Heavens; and I heard again the Voice of many saying—'Blessed be the Glory of the Lord which proceedeth from Him.'

I likewise heard again the motion of the Wings of the Living Ones, and the vibrations of the Wheels as they moved in unison with the Living Ones.

And as the Spirit upbare me, the bitterness of the grief, sorrow and anguish written within the Scroll, filled me till I became one with them.

For the Hand of the Lord was great upon me even to the moving of the Passion of my Being.

Then, in the Firmament that was above the heads of the Cherubim, I beheld the Sapphire Stone that was in fashion like a Throne.

And I heard the Lord God speak unto one who was clothed in fine linen, and say unto him:—

'Move in between the Living Wheels which are under the Cherubim, and fill the hollow of thine hand with the glowing Fire which is between the Cherubim, and scatter the glowing embers of Fire over the City.'

And I saw the one clothed in fine linen go in between the Living Wheels which were beneath the Cherubim.

These stood on the right side of the House when he went in; and the Glory of the Lord filled the Inner Court through the overshadowing Cloud.

Then the Cloud of the Glory of the Lord rose up above the Cherubim, and overshadowed the threshold of the House;

And the whole House became filled with the Radiance of the Lord, from the threshold to the Innermost Court.

The sound of the motion of the Wings of the Cherubim was heard even to the outer court; it was as when the Omnipotent God doth speak.

Then I saw one Cherub put forth his hand from the midst of the Cherubim, and take of the Fire and put it into the hand of him who was garmented with linen.

And he who had received the glowing Fire, went out from the midst of the Wheels which were beneath the Cherubim, and scattered the Fire upon the Earth.

Then I again beheld the four Wheels which accompanied the Cherubim.

They were the colour of Beryl.

Though each Cherub had a Wheel attached to him, yet they all seemed as if they were Wheels within Wheels.

A Glimpse of the Solar Interior

And their motion was fourfold; in their motion they required not to turn round, for they could move in the four directions.

And I heard the Wheels addressed by the Voice of Him who sat upon the Sapphire Throne; for He commanded them in their motion.

And at His command the Wheels unveiled themselves unto me: one had the face of an Angel, another was featured like a Man; one other had the form of Leo in the Celestial Heavens, and the fourth was veiled to sight, for it contained the Mystery of the motion of the Wheels.

Then I saw the Wheels lift up the Cherubim above the Earth: their motion was one, for whithersoever the Wheels went the Cherubim accompanied them. In equipoise and in their fourfold motion, they were as one. For the same Spirit of Life was in them.

Then I witnessed the resplendence of the Lord which filled the threshold withdrawn and passed to the place of the Cherubim; and these rose into the Heavens through the motion of their wings, until they reached the Eastern door of the Divine Sanctuary and stood equipoised beneath the Canopy of the Glory of the God of Israel.

It was like the Vision that came to me when I was by the river Chebar. The forms and motion of the Wheels and Cherubim were the same; and the Glory of the Lord, the God of Israel, was revealed by them as they obeyed His Will and moved according to the motion of the Spirit of Life.

Then the Angel brought me again unto the door of the Eastern Court and shewed me Waters issuing from under the threshold.

These Waters flowed Eastward.

They came from under the right side of the Sanctuary, and flowed from beneath the South side of the Altar.

Then the Angel brought me to the Gate that looked North-ward and led me thence to the outermost Gate which looked Eastward, and behold there ran the Waters which had issued from the right side of the Sanctuary and flowed beneath the South side of the Altar.

Then the Angel, carrying the measuring Rod in his hand, went forth Eastward, taking me with him.

With his Rod he measured 1,000 cubits. And he took me through the Waters; in depth the Waters were up to my ankles.

Then he measured with his Rod 1,000 cubits and took me into the River; the Waters were up to my knees.

After this the Angel stretched forth his Rod and measured another 1,000 cubits. And he took me into the River and through the Waters; here the Waters rose to my loins.

Once more the Angel took me with him as he measured by his Rod yet another 1,000 cubits; but here I found the River so deep that I could not walk through its Waters. The River had become so deep and so great that only those who were great swimmers could enter its Waters. Nor could it be encompassed.

And the Angel said unto me, 'Son of Man, understandest thou this Mystery of God?'

THE LOGIA OF THE MESSAGE

And I was so filled with great Awe at the wonder of the mysterious River, and because of my experiences in its Waters, that the motion of my Being could not find any utterance.

Then I beheld on the banks of the River many Trees. These clothed both sides.

And the Angel said to me, 'Wheresoever these Waters flow, healing is brought to the Earth's streams, and to all Souls.

And the Fruits of the Trees shall be for meat unto all Souls; the Leaves also are of the Everlasting.

And the Fishers of Souls shall sit upon the Banks of the River, from En-gedi even unto En-eglaim.

And the Great Fish shall be found there.'

It came to pass as I sat in the midst of the Seventy Ancients of the House of Israel, that the hand of the Lord God of Israel was laid upon me.

It was within the sixth year, and on the sixth month, and upon the fifth day, that the Vision broke within me.

Before me stood the Lord in the likeness of the Sacred Flame. In appearance He was like Fire from His loins to His feet; and from His loins to His head His appearance was like ineffable Radiance whose light was the colour of pure amber.

He laid His hand upon my head and drew me up out of the earth into His Heavens.

There He opened my understanding and gave me in vision the history of the House of Israel, and of Ierusalem which at one time was the glory of the earth.

I looked through the Northern Gate of the City, and beheld an image which had been fashioned by the spirit of jealousy in those who had wrought great wrongs within Ierusalem; it had been placed at the northern entrance to the Sanctuary, and near the Altar where the Glory of the Lord, the God of Israel, abode.

Then in the outer court of the Sanctuary I beheld how the wall had been breached to make a door other than that which belonged to the Sanctuary; and when I looked through the door, I beheld all the Ancients of Israel.

Each one carried his censer in his hand, and the cloud of incense rose unto the Heavens.

But around them I beheld many things of evil which had been generated by those who had set up the image of jealousy to be worshipped instead of the Lord whose Glory was within the Sanctuary.

These generations were all portrayed upon the wall that was around the court. They were beasts of evil form and desire,

14

ravenous and destructive, and full of the venom of jealousy.

Then the Presence who had upborne me to the place of vision said, 'Behold the darkness caused by the spirit of jealousy! In the midst of it all, the Ancients of Israel had to dwell for many generations.'

Then the spirit bore me to the Northern Gate and bade me look in the Sanctuary. And I beheld many who were as women weeping for their beloved; for Tammuz was dead. The spirit in the image of jealousy had slain him. So the Ancients of Israel mourned for him.

Then the spirit brought me to the inner court of the House of the Lord.

And when I entered by the door of the Sanctuary which was between the North porch and the Altar, I beheld five and twenty men turn their back upon the Altar of the Lord and His overshadowing Glory, though they confessed to having come from the East, and were worshippers of the Sun.

And the Presence spake unto me, saying, 'O, Son of Man! It is no light thing that hath been wrought against the household of Judah; for those who set up the image of jealousy have in very deed filled the land with every kind of abomination, and made the Children of Judah commit in anger deeds of violence; and the spirit in the image of jealousy hath caused ignominy to be heaped upon the Branch of the Lord.'

And as I witnessed all the evil that had been wrought, and the number of the Souls who had been slain by the abominations caused by the spirit of jealousy, I felt as if I alone lived of all the House of Israel; and I fell before the Presence as one overwhelmed, and cried, 'O my Lord, the God of Israel! Save from these abominations the tribes of Ancient Israel!'

15

The Word of the Lord came to me concerning the Prince of Tyrus:

'O Prince of Tyrus, why hast thou lifted up thine heart and laid claim to be as God, reigning in the midst of the Seas as if thou wert God?

Though thou hast set thy heart to be even as God, yet art thou now less than the Son of Man.

Behold how in thy day thou wast wiser than many. No secret was hidden from thee which could bring unto thine understanding the Wisdom of God.

Thou wast enriched with the Silver and Gold of the Treasure-House of God, and many secret things were revealed unto thee.

In thy manifestation thou wast made the sum of Divine Beauty; there was sealed within thee the Wisdom of God.

In the Garden of Eden thou didst walk with Wisdom, and all her precious gems were bestowed upon thee.

The glory of them was thy covering: the Ruby and Sardius, the Topaz and Emerald, the Sapphire and the Amethyst reflected the Radiance of God unto thee.

The Divine Workmanship of all thy qualities accomplished these things for thee in the day when God created thee.

Thou wast anointed of God, one whom the Cherub covered, to be set upon the mountain of God where thou didst walk up and down amid the Sacred Fire.

Thou wast perfect in thy ways from the day of thy manifestation until thou didst go out from the Kingdom that was given unto thee, and from the overshadowing Presence, and so didst fall from thy first estate which was bestowed upon thee within the Garden of God.

Because of the wisdom that was in thee, and all the treasures thou didst possess which were of the Secrets of God, thou didst wield power within the Kingdom appointed unto thee, and thy regnancy gave joy to the Sons of God.

The Kingdom given unto thee was radiant, for the Glory of God filled it.'

*   *   *   *   *

'O Prince of Tyrus!   Behold now the state of the Kingdom that was thine to reign within and administer!

Behold how thy wisdom and thy riches have been changed and become as false knowledge and merchandise!

From the radiance of the Heavens thou hast descended into the great darkness!

From the heights of the mountain of God thou hast fallen into the depths where the discord and violence of evil are made manifest.

Thou knowest no more the joy of the covering Cherub, nor the Glory of God's Overshadowing; for, since thy great betrayal to go out from His Presence Who created and fashioned thee, thou has been a dweller amid the iniquities of those who left their first estate, and who have made of the Holy City of Ierusalem a place where the destroying arrow flieth and the terror doth hold sway.

Thou who didst possess the power that is bestowed from on High by the Highest, art now humbled in the sight of all who should have beheld thy radiance and thy beauty, but who look in vain into the Kingdom where thou didst once reign gloriously, for the revealing of God.

O Prince of Tyrus! though thou hast fallen so far from thy heavenly estate, yet will I Who am thy Lord, cause My Fire to burn within thee, and make all the evil done within thy Kingdom to be consumed away until not even the ashes of the evil remain.

And in that day shall all those who went out with thee also return, and be filled with astonishment at all that I shall cause to be done for thee and for them.'

17

The Word of the Lord came to me when I was dwelling within the City that had been laid waste, even Ierusalem, sorrowing that the Holy City had become so desolated of all that once it had stood for, and that it had now to bear the reproach heaped upon it by those who were strangers to it because they knew not the beauty and the glory with which its Sanctuaries and Palaces were filled before the day in which it also shared in the fall of the Prince of Tyrus.

And the Word of the Lord said unto me,

'Son of Man; hear thou how the Heavens lament over the fall of the Prince of Tyrus, and the City of his one-time glorious reign.

O City, that art situated at the entrance to the Great Sea, the venue for the Souls of many Isles in their search for the riches of Wisdom!

In thy beauty thou wert perfect, even as thy Prince. Those who built thee perfected thy form; and they placed thy borders in the midst of the Great Sea.

Thy vessels of transit were all built out of the Fir-trees of Senir; their uprights were fashioned out of the Cedars of Lebanon.

Bashan formed for thee thy powers of transit, out of the Oak-trees beneath which the sacrifices were offered;

And the companies of the Asshurites formed thy canopies from the sacred woods of Chittim: Egypt supplied thee with fine linen which had been beautifully embroidered, that thine uprights might be able to respond to the Breaths like the sails of a ship to the Winds.

From the Isles of Elishah were given the Blue and the Purple coverings which are in service in the Sanctuaries of the Lord.

THE LOGIA OF THE MESSAGE

Those who served as mariners within the Argosy of thy Kingdom were of ancient Zidon and Arvad; and thy Pilots were all of those who knew the Isles of the Great Sea, and had gathered in of their riches of beauty and wisdom.

The Ancients of Gebal strengthened thee by unifying thine elements; they came in their Argosy upon the Great Sea with their servants and riches.

In thy hosts were found Ancients of Persia, Lud and Phut; these adorned thy walls with their insignia and coverings, and added to the sum of thy beauty.

The dwellers in Arvad sentinelled thy walls, and those of Gammadim thy watch-towers: they ministered of thy come-liness and made manifest thy perfection.

But all this greatness hath been lost, for those who directed thy Argosy brought thee into strange waters. They caused thee to be lost amid the Great Sea.

Again the Word of the Lord came unto me, and I was commanded to set my vision towards Zidon, and declare unto that land the purpose of the Lord, the God of Israel.

Behold, O Zidon! Thus saith the Lord God: 'I will be glorified within thy borders and in the midst of thee; and thy people shall come to know Me as their Lord Whose judgments are holy and not after the manner of those who judge unjustly and without mercy. For they shall be sanctified when My Presence is a Dweller in the midst of them.

In that day there shall be no more any cause of pestilence within thy borders, nor those who defile thy land, nor those slain by their evil ways.

And thou shalt be no more as a thorn to pierce the side of My people, the Ancients of Israel; nor shalt thou harbour those who have despised Me, and rejected those who came from Me to perform My Will in the midst of thee.

For, when I shall have gathered all Israel out of the midst of the peoples amongst whom they have been scattered, and they once more become sanctified for My Service, then they shall dwell again in thy land which I gave unto My Servant Ja-acob-El to rule over, and they shall work in My Vineyard without hindrance or fear, and know that I am in their midst as in the ancient times.'

The Word of the Lord came to me and commanded that I should speak unto the Pharaoh of the Egyptians, and to all his hosts.

'O Pharaoh! Unto whom dost thou liken thyself? Who hath made thee great?

Behold, now, the Assyrian! He was once a Cedar in Lebanon.

His great branches were beautiful, for he dwelt beneath the overshadowing Cloud.

Of great stature was he; he reached into the Cloud of the Glory of the Heavens.

The waters of God nourished him in the midst of the Great Deep, out from whose bosom came he forth to be set up on high.

The streams from on high enriched his roots, as they flowed amongst the trees in the land that was his heritage.

He grew, until in height he overtopped all the other trees of the land; and he extended his branches until he became a cover for many.

His boughs were used as resting-places by all the birds of the Heavens; beneath them the creatures found protection and by them the people knew themselves overshadowed.

Thus was he beautiful in his greatness; his glory was not hidden by the other trees in the Garden of God; nor did any of them envy him.

* * * * *

Consider this, O Pharaoh of Egypt! Why hast thou desired to lift up thyself to the height of that Assyrian, and to spread forth thy branches like his?

To whom dost thou liken thyself in greatness and glory amongst all the trees in the Garden of God?

Behold, now, that which overtook the Assyrian in the day

of his exaltation when he was in the fulness of his greatness and beauty!

The enemy came upon him and threw him down; he was laid low, so his glory departed.

No more can the people dwell beneath his overshadowing branches, nor the creatures find protection, nor the birds of the Heavens resting-places.

The breaths of hell smote all his powers and bore them down unto the nether land.

Great was the mourning for him: the Great Deep, out from whose bosom he came, was sorely troubled because of him; the motion of its waters had to be stayed by the Hand of God.

Lebanon mourned for him in the day of his hurt; and all the Cedars of Lebanon were smitten in his fall.

Those who had grown up with him within the Eden of God went down into the darkness of hell and knew its pains and sorrows.   They became like those who are slain.

All the peoples were shaken by the commotion caused by his fall; for he took them with him in his descent into the abyss.

When he went down into the fearsome pit which the enemy had dug for him, he and all who were with him became over-whelmed in the darkness, amid which they were made to pass through the consuming fires of the nether-world, and bear travail unspeakable.

Since the day of his going down, the Lord God of Israel has very specially had to minister unto all who were of the Cedars of Lebanon, and those who had been in Eden, the Garden of God, to comfort them in their travail with Waters of Life from the streams which flow through the Garden of God.

O Pharaoh of Egypt!   When the Assyrian was exalted to

the Heavens, thou didst also share in his exaltation; but in his fall thou fellest also.

From ruling over a land of rich streams of light and wisdom, thou didst pass to become the ruler of a country amid arid sands desolated with great deserts where the fires of desire burn those who travel across thy highways, and where captivity and oppression are known.

The Fall of Pharaoh and Egypt

Such is the state of the Pharaoh of Egypt to-day.

And with thy descent, O Pharaoh of Egypt, many of the great ones who were the Nobles of the Earth, went down into the nether-parts, drawn down by those who drew thee down into the abyss.

Though thou wert surpassingly beautiful, the enemy caused thee to dwell amidst those who fell from their first high estate.

Asshur is amongst the slain of the Nobles of the Earth. She fell into the pit that had been dug, and found her grave there.

Elam accompanied Asshur. Her Ancients were drawn down and found themselves betrayed ere they knew it, to be enclosed in the prison-houses of the nether-world.

Meshech and Tubal are also there. The enemy overcame them in their warfare with the titanic elemental forces, and cast them into the abyss where the terror had its dwelling.

The dwellers of Edom are all there, the kings and princes of the land; they were slain by the sword of the great enemy who fashioned the abyss and laid snares for the elect of the land.

Zidon was even brought down. Her princes were slain. The Terror overwhelmed them.

O Tyrus! O Zidon! O Egypt! what a time of sorrow when ye went down! And what the travail has since been!'

23

Then I was let down to the planes where dwelt those who were of the Captivity; and I sat me down with them for seven days, full of astonishment at all I had beheld and heard.

And the hand of the Lord touched me and bade me arise and look out upon the planes; and I saw there what I had beheld when I was carried up of the Spirit.

And the Vision overwhelmed me, and I bowed myself unto Him whose Presence stood before me.

Then in my spirit He caught me up, so that I again stood upright before Him.

And He said unto me, 'Son of Man, when thou goest, thou shalt shut thyself within thy House.

And thou shalt lay siege against the enemies of Ierusalem; for they encompass it and besiege it.

In the conquest of the City, thou shalt take upon thy left side the burden of Israel; for upon thy heart must thou bear the iniquity of Israel until the enemy be overthrown and the fulness of days be accomplished.

And upon thy right side must thou take the burden of the iniquity of Judah, and bear it for forty days, until the iniquity of Judah be purged away.

Behold! I have appointed each day.

And until thou hast ended the days of the Siege, and accomplished the conquest of the City, I must put bands (limitations) upon thee, saith the Lord God of Israel, to guard thee.'

THE LOGIA OF THE MESSAGE

The Word of the Lord came unto me and commanded that I should speak unto the Shepherds of Israel. And I spake as the Spirit gave me utterance.

O Shepherds of Israel! Thus saith the Lord God unto you:—

To the
Shepherds
of
Israel

'The woe of the unfaithful has fallen upon you. Of you it has been said that ye eat the riches of the Love and Wisdom of your Lord, yet forget to nourish those who have been impoverished.

The reproach concerning you is that ye have not healed those who have been wounded, nor bound up the broken and maimed, neither have ye strengthened those who have been weakened in the way.

It is even said of you that ye have scattered the sheep and made them easy prey unto the enemy whose emissaries are as ravenous beasts; for the sheep have been without true Shepherds.

O Shepherds of Israel! Why has it come to pass that the enemy of My Flock should find you unguarded as if forgetful of your heritage from your Lord, and your service unto Him?

Behold, saith your Lord! I will search for My sheep until I find them, though they be scattered abroad.

Even as an earthly shepherd seeketh out his flock and gathereth together those that have been scattered, so will I find all My sheep; for I will deliver them out of the hands of the enemy, and bring them back out of the land of darkness.

And I will restore them to the land of Israel, and bring them back into My Pastures; and upon the slopes of the Mountain of God they shall become once more My Flock, and one Fold.

25

And I will give them a Shepherd who will lead them, even David, My Servant, the Beloved one. And he shall be as a Prince of God amongst them, who will, in the Name of the Lord, drive out of the land the beasts of prey that have wrought evil.

He will gather again the Shepherds of Israel unto the high places of blessing upon My Holy Mountain where the rains of the Heavens will lighten upon them.

As the Trees of God in His Garden they will again flourish and bear fruitage; even unto the earthly parts shall come the blessing increasingly.

They shall know hunger no more as in the land of their bondage, nor the shame which the oppressors heaped upon them; for the Glory of their Lord shall be upon them, and they will become renowned as His Shepherds.

And it shall be made manifest that the Lord God of Sabaoth is with them.'

The Lord laid His Hand upon me in blessing; and He bare me up in the motion of the Spirit.

And He opened my vision and revealed to me the state of the whole of the House of Israel.

And He likewise made known unto me His Holy Purpose concerning Israel in the land of Judah.

In my vision I beheld a valley peopled with the dead, as if a multitude had been slain in it, for the valley seemed to be full of the remains of the dead.

In the open champaign everything appeared to be very dry, as if the Breath of Life were absolutely absent.

The Voice of the Presence spake to me saying, 'Son of Man, thinkest thou these dead can live again?'

And I answered, 'O my Lord, Thou Who art the Lord God of Israel alone knowest.'

Then was I instructed what to prophesy concerning the restoration of the whole House of Israel.

O ye dead within the valley of death, hear ye the Voice of the Lord your God; for thus speaketh He:—

'Behold! I will cause the Breath to blow through the valley, and ye shall live again.

I will clothe your bones with sinews, and your sinews with flesh, and your flesh with a covering; and will cause the Breath to fill you, and ye shall live and again know Me as your Lord.'

Now as I prophesied, a great sound broke the stillness. It was the coming to life of those who had been dead. Bone came to bone in unity, and sinew to sinew, and the covering of all parts with flesh and skin.

Then did I hear the Voice speak to the Four Breaths, saying, 'Come now, O Breath, and breathe from the four quarters of the Heavens upon those who have been dead, that they may live again.'

And the Breath from the four dimensions moved within them and made them live again.

And they arose and stood upon their feet marshalled as Hosts of the Lord.

Then spake the Voice unto me, saying, 'These are the whole House of Israel. And they say "Our very bones are lacking in marrow, and are dry; and our hope of Salvation has grown dim. We are as those who are put away."

Therefore, Son of Man, say unto them, 'Thus saith the Lord God of Hosts, O Israel My people, how cometh it to pass that ye have forgotten Me?

Behold, once more shall I come unto you, and the graves wherein ye were laid shall deliver you up, and the enemy who put you in them shall be overthrown;

For I shall again make My Name glorious in your midst.

The Waters from the Fountain of Life will I pour out upon you, and ye shall be cleansed from the stain of the evil that overtook you.

The Heart will I again cause to beat in unison with My Will; for I will renew its substance.

My Spirit once more will I cause to move within you, that ye may be upborne and able to walk before Me to fulfil My Statutes and learn anew My Secrets, and from henceforth dwell in the realm of My Presence, even the patriarchal land which was thine in the ancient times.

And I will tabernacle in the midst of you; and the children of Judah shall come to know that the Lord God of Hosts is in the midst of Israel.

Thus shall I make manifest through Israel the Glory of My Name.'

THE MESSAGE OF EZEKIEL

A COSMIC DRAMA

*

Part Two

*

THE OFFICE OF A PROPHET

THE OFFICE OF A PROPHET

A true Prophet is the Servant of the Most High. He is not a resultant of human education, for no scholastic centre could endow him with more than human knowledge. If scholastic colleges and ecclesiastic seminaries could have bestowed such a gift upon their students, assuredly this world would have been the home of vast communities of true Prophets.

Thus-wise a Prophet is not made. He is GOD's direct creation. He is God-begotten, fashioned and illumined. A Prophet is one who has taken Divine Masonic degrees in the Heavens. In his Being he has ascended from one state of spiritual consciousness to another, growing in spiritual attribute through his contact with Angels and Gods until he has attained the status of *an Illumined one*. In this exalted inward state he can receive Divine Illumination and communicate it: he can henceforth fill the office of Divine Prophet.

Such an office implies universal sympathy. Though the Prophet will derive his personal equation through family and race, yet he will transcend these; for to be dominated by the thought of family, tribe and race would place the prophet under great limitation. And that could not be if his sphere of illumination were associated with the realm of Universal Being, and his message to the Eternal and the Soul. For the message given him to proclaim would be of universal import which would necessitate the transcension by him of the limited bounds created by personal, national and racial relationships. And herein will his message exceed in significance and scope and differ from that of many who might be regarded as prophets, but whose message is related to the prophet's own people or race.

These latter are minor Prophets indeed. The true great Prophets have a message of universal value, and speak of

Soulic, Celestial, and Divine Events. Therefore, it should not be difficult to differentiate between the messages of the true Prophets because of their universal significance, and those who are merely political and national enthusiasts, denouncing at times their own people, and upon other nations pouring forth judgments. It will be readily conceded by students of the prophetic books of the Old Testament, that there are two orders of prophetic utterances found in those books, the one relating to what could only be accounted local and national, and the other to themes and events of transcendent nature, themes relating to the Mysteries of Planetary, Celestial and Divine history, and of great Soulic value.

It is in the light of such revelations when these are fully unveiled, that the message of the real Prophet of GOD is distinguished from the most mixed addenda of the writings of the local and national teachers (though bearing the name of prophets), introduced by the various scribes, editors and redactors, and mixed up with the true Divine Message to the latter's obscuration. For it was in this way that the ancient Scribes and Pharisees made void the Law and the Testimony from GOD given unto and through HIS illuminated ones.

MESSAGES TRUE AND FALSE

True prophetic messages are written in cryptic terms. They are something more than interpretations given to local and national religious ideas. The message of a true Prophet is something profoundly greater and loftier than any statements that are imbued with the spirit of national political bias and racial religious prejudices. Of these latter the books of the Old Testament are full. They are to be found side by side with the real Message and are the work of the priestly scribes. And this must be borne in mind if the reader of the Old Testament prophecies would discern between the true and the false, the illumined message of the illumined Soul and that message in a false setting, changed and placed there to support traditional beliefs of a local, national or racial character. Jewry claimed the Prophets and Seers, and these were made to speak for Jewry. The JEHOVAH Who reveals HIMSELF unto the Prophets and Seers as the Most Holy and transcendent ONE, *who filleth all things*, is so changed into an anthropomorphic GOD that HE becomes one with like passions and humours as possessed the people. To the real Prophet HIS is an unchanging Love; but to Jewry HE is ever changing towards them with every change in the religious or national life. HIS mercy flies like a radiant cloud across the Heavens, followed soon by clouds of judgment. Though the most sacred Name by which HE was known in Israel became known to Jewry because it belonged to the terms used in the Mysteries which came into their possession, yet the most glorious ONE Whose Name was above all earthly names and was signified by the Tetragrammaton, was reduced to the conception of an eastern potentate who reflected in himself the changing emotions, desires, ambitions, loves and hates of the nation's own fallen states.

The deep shadow of such a tragedy as this degradation of the Divine Nature, Love and Wisdom, lies athwart the threshold of all the prophetic Books of the Old Testament.

THE PROPHET ILLUMINED OF GOD

The true Prophet was an illumined Soul, and his message was an illumination. Being illumined of GOD the message he had to give could not misrepresent the Divine Nature, Love and Wisdom. In such a message there would be nothing derogatory to the Divine Love and Wisdom.

Whatever the nature of the message, it would always be of transcendent character and worthy of HIM concerning Whom it spake. To know the Divine Presence even in the degree in which a true Prophet must know that glorious ONE, would ensure that the Prophet could not represent HIM as if HE were like a man, governed by the changing degrees of desire and passion characteristic of fallen humanity.

In the real message of the true Prophet, the LORD, the GOD of Sabaoth, was as unlike the representation of HIM in the denunciatory parts of the prophetic Books, as the transcendent glory of a perfect day is unlike the deep darkness of the night wherein not even a star shines to relieve its gloom. Unto the true son of Israel who had risen into the realm of high illumination and become GOD's Prophet, the LORD GOD of Sabaoth was also the LORD of the Inner Sanctuary and the Shekinah overshadowing the Soul's shrine. HE was the Voice whose vibration spoke of Love and Wisdom, compassion and pity. Yet, through the misrepresentations of HIM by the teachers and priests, the people of Jewry dreaded HIM. HE was thought of as ONE whose demands, laws and statutes were inwrought with judgments and punishments, and Who wrested obedience from HIS children by the elementary means of promises of rewards for obedience, and sufferings for disobedience.

THE CRYPTIC LANGUAGE OF THE PROPHET

The transcendent Visions and Messages found in the Old Testament are the true prophetic Teachings. They are often cryptographic; and frequently hieroglyphs are used to set them forth. For the innermost Mysteries conveyed in the messages had to be guarded from those who would have wrested them and put the knowledge to wrong uses, with the danger of bringing disaster upon themselves and others, and even upon the Planet, as had been in other ages when great minds made wrong use of the knowledge of Planetary secrets, and caused great catastrophes to befall the elements, seas and outer planes. That is the reason why in the prophetic Books the innermost Mysteries were presented in the language of glyph, so that only the illumined could come into the true knowledge of them.

This Divine provision accentuates in all the Books of the Old Testament the difference between the message of the real Prophet of GOD Who was the medium of the revelation of the Mysteries, and the local and national so-called prophet whose interests were chiefly Jewish, and very often only tribal and personal. In the Old Testament the contrast between the voice of the true Prophet and that of the priestly Scribe is most obvious from Isaiah to Malachi, and even long before the books which bear their names became part of the Jewish Canon. The two voices have different messages, and these are mostly at variance. That of the true Prophet calls to the Inner Life, and deals with the Mysteries of the Heavens and the Earth, GOD and the Soul, the Sun and the Planet; that of the priestly Scribe calls to obedience to outer temple-ceremonial and ritual, and emphasizes the Divine necessity and value of these. The true Prophet is not oblivious of the beautiful outer aspects of religious expression, but he sees the danger of these when unaccompanied by Divine illumination and consecration. He knows that where the innermost significances of the Mysteries are apprehended and applied, the outer worship will express the inner beauty and glory of Life. But the mere tribal, national and racial priest and scribe, see not the inner relationships to the outward ritual and ceremonial. To them the former may be experienced by the few; whilst the latter must be observed by all. Yet the office of the true Prophet and that of the true Priest is of the sublime Mystery of GOD, and should ever have been in harmony; and the outer ceremonial and ritual should always have been the articulation of the inner motion of the Divine Spirit and the shadowing forth of the Mysteries.

* * * * * *

Prophecy is usually associated with the prediction of coming events in the immediate or distant future. The prophetic is here brought down from its realm of exalted spiritual vision to that of the occult or even the astral realm. Many who are far from the state of spiritual consciousness necessary for the true Prophet, and who could not possibly fill his office, have nevertheless been able to foretell coming events upon the outer planes. Many of the things foretold whose action is upon the outer planes may be known beforehand because they are the results of activities upon the astral and occult planes. Very few clairvoyants see beyond these planes; and it is there that outward events are shadowed forth. On the higher occult plane many render beautiful ministries; and there are times when those who minister there are permitted to communicate what may have been seen or heard. Most of the spiritualistic experiences and communications through mediums are from that plane.

Such experience and communications are, however, very different in nature and character from those which are the outcome of true prophecy and the office of the true Prophet. The Prophet of GOD does not function within the astral and occult realms. His office is of such a nature that he is borne aloft in his consciousness far beyond the realms of the ordinary medium. He shares the motion of the realms of the true spiritual and angelic life and ministry. He hears the Voices of the Inner World, and communes with Angels and even Archangels. His Message is from the Divine: the Voice of the Eternal ONE makes all his planes vibrate and respond to the Divine motion. The Four Breaths move through him; the Four Living Creatures or Divine Atmospheres within him are the recipients of the Breath. His Rings, or Wheels, or Planes (they are the same), go whithersoever the Spirit goeth; and they are full of Eyes or the light of heavenly perception. The cherubic motion of which he speaks he will understand, his knowledge of it will be through cherubic motion in himself.

UNDERSTANDING THE SIGNS AND SYMBOLS

When the Message of the true Prophet is understood, the interpretation of the hieroglyphs will throw light upon the world's darkness. It will unveil the Divine Drama of the Soul, reveal the meaning of the Earth's tragedies and the Soul's travail, and interpret the Divine Purpose. And to understand the Message even after the hieroglyphs are interpreted and the cryptic signs uncovered, the seeker must approach in reverence and from the standpoint of the spiritual realms. No mere textual criticism, however valuable it may be accounted from the traditional or scholastic standpoint, can possibly give an insight into the Divine significance of the Message. Indeed, textual criticism has not only missed the mark in failing to effect what was hoped for from it, but the critics have closed the doors to many of the entrants who would fain come into a knowledge of the Divine and Celestial Mysteries set forth in the prophetic Books   The spirit of hyper-criticism has often prevented the scholar from entering into the kingdom whence the Vision and the Message of the Prophet have come; and it has left unopened the gates to the Temple of the Mysteries, and thus failed in its ministry to those who have desired to enter into the Divine Pantheon of prophetic Revelation. Ultra-criticism has not provided the Realities for all who have earnestly sought the truth; but it has shaken the foundations of religious belief in many. It has not thrown light upon the way into the Kingdom of GOD; alas! it has only too often obscured the inner vision of those who have brought the criticism of the mind to bear upon things essentially of the Soul and the Divine Kingdom.

* * * * * *

There is only one way of approach to the true understanding of the messages of the divinely inspired and illumined Prophets. It is the path of Soul enlightenment. *But all enlightenment is from within.* Knowledge gained from without informs the mind, but it does not enlighten the Being. Many have held the Mysteries in the cryptographic body of their presentation without finding the inner meaning of them. For witness to this we have the Christian Church of to-day that holds its Seven Sacraments as the Mysterious Rites by which the Soul of man finds GOD; yet the Church has no real illumination concerning the Divine Soul significance of each Sacrament. Of each Sacrament it makes a masonic rite of great import to the individual; and it does this even whilst it condemns all masonic rites expressive of the Mysteries, if these are rendered outside of its own communion. By the path of illumination the Mysteries become Revelation to the true seeker. The terms in which the Mysteries are expressed are the various masonic Signs, Symbols and Passwords contained within the degrees in their ascending scale. Each Mystery is a cryptograph; each term a cryptogram.

Such was the character of the true prophetic Teachings.
Of such character may those Teachings be seen to be now
by all who come into the realm of light. These Teachings
contain Divine Secrets. The Secrets had to be guarded.
They had to be protected from those who sought knowledge
for personal ends, who would wrest nature's secrets from
her for personal ambitious purposes, and make use of
them to dominate and conquer. For it was through such
a misuse of the secret potencies of the Planet that many
great disasters befell the Earth's outer planes. And such
minds would also wrest from the Soul of man its Divine
Secret; for which reason the Mysteries concerning the
constitution of the Soul have been veiled from all but those
who attain to the Divine Consciousness.

The Teachings of the true Prophets were related to the
Divine Kingdom and contained illuminations on

The Secrets of Creation:

The constitution and fashion of the Earth:

The nature and place in the Heavens of the Solar
Body:

The creation, fashioning and evolution of the
Sons of GOD:

The creation and generation of the Children of
this world:

The fall of this Planet and, in some degree, as a
result, the whole system;

The primary cause of "the Fall," and the disastrous
results to the whole Planetary Household, to the
Sons of GOD, and to all those who caused it to
take place:

The ministry of the Divine World with a view to
effecting the Planet's restoration:

The nature of those ministries which had to undergo

39

change from time to time because of the new
unforeseen difficult conditions which arose:

The tragic things which befell the outer planes of
the Planet and all the races upon them:

The rending of the Planet's Kingdoms, written of
under the guise of the Kingdom of Judah and
the Kingdom of Israel:

The Divine Purpose expressed in the coming of the
Messengers, and very specially in the Messianic
Advent revealed in and through the Master
known as Jesus Christ:

The nature of the Redemption to be accomplished
on behalf of the Sons of GOD who bore the
cryptograms of Israel and Zion:

The effect of that Redemption upon the Kingdoms
and planes of the Planet, and upon all her
children:

The path of the Oblation, its nature, burden and
duration:

The resultant of the Oblation revealed in the
Regeneration of the Sons of GOD and their
restoration to their long lost Divine Inheritance:

The rehabilitation of the Ancient Christhood, and a
corporate Messianic Manifestation through restored Israel:

The ultimate triumph of the Divine Love and
Wisdom over all the fallen astral and occult
forces and conditions, and the re-establishing of
the Christ-regnancy in the restoration of the
ancient Theocracy.

Such is the burden of the Teachings of the true Prophets.
These Teachings constitute the Great Mysteries of the
ages. They are gems of Revelation which have been over-
laid by their settings, hidden beneath priestly ceremonial

and national traditions, and the local, tribal and racial application of them to Jewry. Even the apparently personal names assigned to the Books are cryptic, and indicate the subject-matter of the Revelation. The understanding of the terms is the "open sesame" to the hidden truth. These terms have no more relation to the Prophet-servant of the LORD, than had the sacred terms Jesus Christ the Lord to the personal Master, though the terms were given to Him as personal names, notwithstanding that the real meaning of them is found in His Mission. And thus with the true Prophets. The Servant took the term signifying the Office. To analyse the Names of the Prophets in relation to the Message which they were appointed to give, is interesting and illumining. Thus: (*See page 42*).

All this will indicate the wealth of sacred story that came into the hands of Jewry through the Schools of the Prophets. Alas! the Scribes and Priests did not understand the inner meaning of the various messages. They misinterpreted them, with the result that often their misrepresentations were accepted as the real message, and chronicled as such. Thus the real vision was veiled by them, and the true Treasure buried amidst the elements of their own national and racial history.

Yet the Messages of all the Prophets, Major and Minor, make up one grand Symphony of Divine Revelation of Motion, Purpose, Travail and accomplishment on the part of the Divine World on behalf of Israel and Judah.

THE MESSAGE OF EZEKIEL

THE PROPHETIC BOOKS

THE MESSAGE	NAME	MEANING OF NAME
The Drama of the Oblation	Isaiah or Ye-shá-yah	The Burden of the Spirit of Jehovah
The Divine Lament over Israel, Judah and Ierusalem	Jeremiah or Je-remai-yah	The appointed of Jehovah
An Unveiling of Planetary History	Ezekiel	In whom is Divine Strength
A History of Israel in Allegory	Daniel	The Divine Judge or Separator
The Flight of the Beloved	Jonah	The Dove or the Beloved One
The Way of Salvation	Hosea	The Saviour
A Divine Reveillé	Joel	Jehovah is the Lord
The Travail of the Planet-Soul	Amos	The Burden-bearer
The Way into the Holiest	Micah or Michiyah	Jehovah is our Strength
Assurance of the overthrow of the Great City (Nineveh)	Nahum	A Son of Consolation
Counsel concerning guarding the Message of God	Zephaniah	Jehovah is our Guardian
The Process of Regeneration	Habakkuk	Divine Embracement
The Overthrow of Edom and Esau	Obadiah	Worship God only
The Coming of Triumph	Haggai	The Feast of Yahweh
The Sanctuary Restored	Zechariah	The Divine Omniscience
The Refiner's Fire	Malachi	The Messenger of Yahweh

42

THE MESSAGE OF EZEKIEL

A COSMIC DRAMA

★

PART THREE

★

THE PURPORT OF THE BOOK

THE PURPORT OF THE BOOK

The Prophet who bears the name of Ezekiel has left us a monumental work. It is a book that few read with an open understanding of the Revelation contained. The language is strange, the imagery often Babylonian, the meaning of the visions not easy to apprehend. Scholars and commentators acknowledge the difficulties in the way of giving a truly satisfactory and coherent interpretation of the various visions. Except that it concerns itself with the captivity of Judah and Israel, the return from captivity and the resurrection of the whole House of Israel, the Book would appear to have no high illuminations full of Revelation concerning both the land of Judah and all her children, and the past history of Israel.

Yet it is a Book of great Illumination and Revelation.

The Prophecy is concerned with Planetary History, and with Judah in relation to that History, past, present and to come. In the Prophet's vision, the Children of Israel are a distinct people, a quite different race from the Children of Judah, a community of Souls who had committed to them a great ministry unto Judah which, through Planetary changes, had been intercepted, and they themselves brought down into bondage and afflicted cruelly by many oppressors, and even by those whom they sought to serve.

The Prophecy opens with a Celestial Vision. It is so transcendent that the Prophet finds it difficult to express what he saw and heard. He beholds things Divine under the imagery of Living Wheels, the motion of which was controlled and directed by the Spirit of the LORD. Whithersoever the Spirit directed, the Wheels moved in obedience. In the midst of them there was a Chariot made up of Cherubim, and upon the Cherubic Chariot sat One whose appearance was as Living Fire. He had motion also like a lambent Flame, and he moved amongst the Rings and Wheels.

Moving with these were four Living Creatures. They had six wings, like those in the Apocalyptic vision and the Seraphim in motion in Isaiah's vision. They are said to have had four faces each—those of an Angel, an Eagle, a Lion, and an Ox.

The whole vision is not only of Divine order and related to the Celestial realms, but it is also intimately connected with the Planet. The nature and constitution of the Planet is unveiled. The motion of the Rings and Wheels reveals the fashion of the Planet and the motion of its interior planes as these were constituted in the unfallen days. The lambent Flame is the Divine Mystery who is said to be a consuming Fire, and is the unveiling of the Secret Power at the heart of the Planetary constitution.

These four images or faces have been taken to represent the four Kingdoms and their corresponding vehicles of manifestation—the physical, the astral, the higher mental, and spiritual. They have also been applied by writers on the Gospels to the four Records. Matthew has had assigned to his story the Ox, as representing the Jewish people, as his Gospel is considered essentially Jewish. Mark has had given to his record the symbol of the Lion, because his Gospel is concerned with power, and has been named the Roman Gospel. To Luke has been assigned the Angel, because his Gospel is so essentially Human, and in its composition is like the Greek Divine Human concept. With John has been associated the Eagle because of that bird's power to soar, and the Gospel attributed to John partakes so much of the nature of the Son of GOD, its flights so often being to the Divine World.

Then there are those who relate the four faces to the Elemental Kingdoms over which GOD reigns, the Cherubim being elemental Spirits whose motion is revealed in and through the living Rings and Wheels; and also that those Kingdoms form the path of evolution for the Soul. Symbolically they are interpreted as representing Patience, Power, Flight, and Soul attainment.

But these four forms are symbols of the Four Living Creatures in the Apocalyptic vision. They are related to the Four Eternities. The Four Eternities are mystical expressions to indicate the Divine Motion through the Four Divine Kingdoms as represented by our Earth terms, North, South, East, and West. And these Four Eternities speak of the four degrees of Divine manifestation, and the four great Ascensions which all who dwell within the consciousness of the Divine Kingdom must take.

Proceeding from the Divine World, these four unveil the realms of the Divine Motion, the magnetic outflow of the Divine Love and Wisdom of which the Angel speaks, the upbearing flight of the Holy Spirit when that most Holy ONE enters into the realm of Divine Elements to set them in motion and give them increased potency for manifestation.

Proceeding from the Kingdom of the Soul these four express the realms of experience, acquisition, ascension, and realization. By experience the Soul learns patience and endurance. In the manifest world and universe it acquires knowledge which, when changed by application, becomes dynamic force. Thus it gains in potency to make its ascensions through the Four Kingdoms and enter the Divine World. For the Soul must gather into itself the potencies by the possession of which it is enabled to proceed through the Eternities, even until it becomes one with the Divine.

With this exalted vision of the Divine Kingdom, as that sublime realm was expressed in the World unfallen, the Prophet proceeds to unveil the fallen state of the Planet and the powers that brought it low. To the Prophet, the captivity in Babylon is a spiritual event. The Brook Chebar upon whose banks the vision breaks upon him, is a mystical river, and the plains, hills and mountains are of like quality. Many states are named under the imagery of cities, rulers and peoples, and their connection with the fall of the whole Planetary Constitution is unveiled. It is true, and obvious to any mystical student, that the terms containing the secret of the betrayal and fall of this Earth are cryptic, and that they require a Key to unlock the door for entrance into the Book of Divine Mysteries. But when once the Seer enters into the Temple of prophetic imagery, there pass before him in dioramic fashion, the story of the betrayal of this world, the titanic battle of the elements as these were controlled and directed by those who understood the Planetary Constitution, who should have remained the servants of the Most High and fulfilled His Will, but who desired to found a new Celestial Dynasty whose embodiments would have most of their elements in a fixed state wherein they would be in such bondage that they could not respond magnetically to the Divine Law of motion as that Law operated within that realm. These conflicts are presented under guise of outward history, the fall of Ierusalem, the conquest of Judah by the Babylonian rulers, the captivity of all Judah's

Children, the heavy burdens imposed upon the House of
Israel and their sore travail; the Divine Siege of Ierusalem
and how the burden of the captivity of both Judah and
Israel was borne; the fall of the Prince of Tyrus from his
former high estate and the spoliation of his once famous
city of Tyrus; the change that was effected in the one-time
famous city of Zidon with the descent of her Princes and
all the Zidonians; the change that overcame the Assyrian
who grew up in Eden and rose to be greater than many of
the Trees of Eden in estate, and attained to the Cloud of
Glory in the Heavens, but who fell from the summit of
his greatness through self-exaltation, and brought down
with him the whole of the House of the Prince of Egypt,
and who went down into the netherworld, taking with him
many of the Ancients and those in the intermediary
realms.

This is followed by a Divine forecasting of the results of
the Oblation wherein there would be a restoration of the
Earth's Kingdoms and all those who went down into the
abyss; the reconstitution of the realms of the Princes of
Zidonia, Tyrus, Assyria and Egypt, with the return of all
who went down into captivity.

The Divine Drama then concerns itself with Israel.
Their restoration to the estate of Princes of Eden, the land
of their Inheritance, was to be an essential number in the
solution of the problem of the Planet's Redemption, for
they were Children who had the inheritance of the
Ancients. The Prophet saw them after *the great diaspora*
when they became scattered upon the planes of the Earth
and no longer active as the Ancients, but rather as those
who have been slain by the enemies who betrayed them
and brought them down into the valley of humiliation
where they found the conditions of the abyss.

THE MESSAGE OF EZEKIEL

In his Divine Drama the Prophet sees them all restored and become once more the Host of the LORD. As such a vehicle of Divine Potency, they witness once more the flow of the Divine Stream from beneath the Altar within the Holy Temple, whose waters in their Divine accommodation meet the needs of all Souls, and bring healing to them and the elements of the Earth. As a result the once Holy City of Ierusalem is restored to her former glory wherein the stranger to the Divine way of Life no longer walks, but where everything pure and true and righteous obtains and prevails.

In such a City the Temple of GOD may once more be fully reared for Divine Ministries, the Priesthood which is of GOD be re-instituted, the Cloud of Radiance again over-shadow the Sanctuary, and the most sacred sacrifice of the Host of the GOD of Sabaoth be offered.

Such are the contents of this most marvellous prophetic story-book, presented under glyph and cryptograph so that none but the illuminated might discern, and not even these latter until *the Oblation had been accomplished and the Book of its Mystery could be unsealed, and the Divine Drama of this world could be unveiled.*

50

THE MESSAGE OF EZEKIEL

A COSMIC DRAMA

*

PART FOUR
A

*

A TRANSCENDENT VISION—
THE DIVINE WORLD UNVEILED

THE DIVINE WORLD UNVEILED

Ezekiel is said to have been a Priest, and one of the captivity. Only a Priest of the Inner Sanctuary could possibly have beheld the visions that came to him. They are chronicled by him in cryptographic language because the real message could be presented only in hieroglyph. It could be understood only by the children whom the LORD illumined. It was meant to convey much to the Sons of GOD, to restore a vision whose light was of HIS own glorious resplendence.

The book, though retained in the canon of the Old Testament scriptures, has been a problem to scholars through the ages. Even the Jewish people who have in a very special way claimed those Old Scriptures as their peculiar possession, have been so deeply disturbed at times by the message of Ezekiel, that it has frequently been a consideration with their scholars whether it should have a place amidst their other sacred writings. The Christian Church has received the book into the canon because of its intrinsic value, especially in relation to the call of the Divine unto the Soul and the individual life responsibility, which is very clearly set forth in some intermediary chapters; and also because there is a description (at least it is so taken to be) of the rebuilding of the temple.

Concerning the cryptographic parts, however, with their wonderful illuminative glyph, the book appears to be of no value whatever to the Christian Church, and might well not belong to the canon. Yet, strange to say, it is in those very cryptic parts where the most sacred Mysteries are revealed. The book is believed to deal with the House of Israel, in chief, though also with that of Judah. Very especially does it deal with the distinction given to Israel and with Israel's supposed declension; with the Divine

Lord's address to His people, and the subsequent return and restoration of Israel. There are four great divisions which I would fain look at with you, in so far as that may be possible. They are these:—

1. The Transcendency of God;

2. The Mystery of Divine Formation, Motion, and Ministry, as represented in the Wheels and the Living Creatures;

3. The distinction held by Israel in the land of Judah;

4. The Resurrection of Israel;

5. The restoration of the Temple Service with the glorious Priesthood of Israel which was to become the exposition of the Kingdom of God—God incarnate in the corporate body of Israel, and through the individual life of each member of the Christhood.

I

THE TRANSCENDENCY OF GOD

Some things are not easy to express, so you may find it difficult to follow me; but I hope it may be possible to present them with clarity sufficient to make them obvious to you. These deal with the Secrets of God in the Soul, in the Planet, and in the Universe. For the Secrets relate to a Celestial system, to the Sons of God, to the Household of Israel, and to an individual Soul who is so endowed that there is possessed the capacity to cognize God as present in all things. For by a most glorious ascending arc of evolutionary motion accomplished by manifold stages, and the growth by means of the expansion and deepening of consciousness, the Soul at last can know Him, can endure to enter into the realm of consciousness where He is realized. For in such a state the Soul not only cognizes

HIM as manifested in all HIS works, not only feels HIM as a Presence with the life, but is conscious of HIM as the indwelling Presence and as ONE Who can be so realized that the whole Being becomes interfused by the streams which flow from HIS own glorious centre, by means of which the Soul is so uplifted as to be able to dwell in the consciousness of that ONE, evermore living in HIM, moving in HIM, having all the Being's experience in desire, motion and vision, in HIM, from HIM, and always for HIM:—this is what is presented in that opening chapter of the book of Ezekiel. This is what is presented in the Text in the restored transcription.

Recently an article appeared in one of the papers bearing this strange title: "This terrible universe in which we dwell." It was written by a scientist. It had its origin in his thought and its expression through his pen, as the result of the planetary conditions which have been prevailing during these latter days. The strange seismic action and the volcanic activity have brought physical scientists face to face with problems which none of their solvents can resolve. A true scientist is one who knows. Therefore his deductions should be correct. They would not be dependent on uncertain deductions from apparent phenomena. They would have their foundation in the knowledge of the cause which produces the phenomena.

Other contemporaneous articles have been written which might well fill the children of the FATHER-MOTHER with dismay, and impress them with the thought that they were in the midst of a universe where blind force practically obtained and prevailed, where accidents of tremendous nature might happen any day, and the world itself be broken to pieces and destroyed with all its children.

It must needs be in this world, and in some other

members of the family of this system, that great changes take place in the outer planes, because of the processes that are at work at the heart of the various members. And especially am I thinking of the Earth. It must needs be that volcanic action continues until there is cast out of the intermediary spheres the elements which should never have been there; and that seismic activity should express itself in tidal waves and earthquakes, not because the Divine Love and Wisdom orders these, but because of that hidden mysterious motion of the inner planes of the Planet which is absolutely necessary for the restoration of the Planet to be once more as a redeemed land, a balanced world, a restored home. For originally this Earth was a glorious system of Human Souls. And these are to be brought back to the beautiful estate of life which obtained in earlier ages when all the conditions were truly Edenic, and the higher spiritual aspects of life and service were most beautiful, when the elder children were taught by the Sons of GOD how to attain to that estate of life wherein they would not only cognize GOD in the things around them, but be conscious of HIS Presence with them.

* * * * * *

It is of the Divine World Ezekiel has to speak in the opening vision of the motion within the Divine World, which has also the corresponding motion in a world like this, in perfect estate. True, he has mostly to speak of this world in its fallen estate, and also how the healing of the world is to be accomplished and the whole of its household brought back once more into that estate of life wherein paradise shall obtain amongst them, and the Edenic state which is the beatific estate, the most blessed estate of the Soul, fill the heart with the very joy of life. For the Prophet knew that such a life as we have, with all its sacred Mystery and its marvellous attributes, with its

Divine potencies and its most heavenly motion, should be a joyous life—a life whose cup was filled with the Joy of Being. And herein the Prophet expressed the Life of the Heavens. For, to be the children of the FATHER-MOTHER should surely be upon the earth, even as it is in the Heavens, a Divine Joy. It could not be the Will of the FATHER-MOTHER that life should be one long travail wherein the waters of joy were changed into waters of Marah and Sinim, or Soul bitterness.

THE CHARIOT OF FIRE

Now, you will come with me into those inner realms of which the Prophet speaks, that we may look at the Transcendency of the FATHER-MOTHER amidst HIS creation. There is a formulated description of HIM. HE is presented in the fashion of the Divine Man that the mind may apprehend sufficiently when the truth is unveiled. The Divine Man is in the heart of the Sacred Flame. The Flame proceeds from HIS loins. That is a term used to describe the Divine or Solar centre of the Being. The Flame moves upwards and envelops HIM. It moves downward and envelops HIM. By that is meant that it moves through the Heavens of the Being; it moves through the worlds of HIS creation.

The sacred Flame is the sacred Fire you read of in occult story; the sacred Fire which is the symbol of the Mystery of Divine Energy in the universe, in all worlds, in all Souls. It is the Chariot of Fire. For the Throne beheld by the Prophet became as a chariot upon which was seated the Eternal ONE, but figured unto the vision as the Divine Man. Around HIM stood the Cherubim and the Seraphim. Before HIM and about HIM were the Four Living Creatures. We will see presently what these signify. When HE spake they had motion, and their motion was toward HIM and from HIM.

57

This motion of Living Forces represented the creative processes in the Divine World; those processes as they proceed in Celestial generation and the formation of worlds; and also the procedure of the same processes in the generation of Human Souls. For the Human Soul has within itself all that the Prophet saw in his vision. It has within its system, microcosmically expressed, the Cherubim and the Seraphim and the Four Living Ones. Language fails the Prophet for adequate expression, so he has to have resource to figurative speech even though it hides the meaning to such an extent that the Soul has to discover it.

THE FOUR DIMENSIONS

We will now unveil such parts as may be revealed that you may be able to proceed unto the vision of which it speaks, but which is to be found alone in the realization of the sublime truth. For the Four Living Ones express the motion of the Four Eternities. The Four Eternities represent the four Divine Dimensions—the East and the West, the North and the South. These are not geographical situations such as we apply the terms to on the Earth. They represent great Spiritual, Celestial, and Divine Qualities. HE Who is the ETERNAL GOD operates through the fourfold Eternities. It is the motion of the Eternal Mystery—creative and formulative, endowing unto the western manifestation, as that expression applies to the Divine World and the Celestial Universe, and as it relates even to our own life. For the East of our life is the Orient where the Light of GOD abides and whence it proceeds in ever-increasing splendour, until it floods the whole Being through shedding its glory into every part of it.

Now in relation to this I would have you observe that it proceeds through the action of the Divine Presence upon the magnetic poles of the Being, which poles are represented by the North and the South. The northern magnetic pole is that which becomes acted upon through the Overshadowing of the Divine Presence. The southern pole is the negative of the northern. Through the dual action, the centrifugal and the centripetal, the positive and the negative, or (to translate the idea into the ordinary human speech) the masculine and the feminine modes, we have as a resultant the Divine Overshadowing of the Soul; and this so enriches it, not only unto manifesting through a form, but so enriches it that the whole Being ultimately becomes a manifestation of the Eternal Mystery seen by the Prophet in the Divine World. For there is within and around the Being where the LORD Presence sits upon the throne of the Kingdom of the Soul, the motion of Cherubim and Seraphim and the ministry of the Four Living Ones. There burns the sacred Fire. The Flame of that Fire flows upward and downward through the Spiral of the Being.

All Souls in their superstructure are made like the Heavens themselves. Each one is a Spiral. Each one contains within himself and herself the Eternities. If you did not contain the correspondence you could never get there. You could never contact them, never understand them to such fulness that you could dwell in the consciousness of them. Each one has Seraphic power for the outflow of Soul ministry. Each one has Cherubic power for the inflow of the Being's ministry. Each one thus represents the Divine Mystery. *That is the meaning of man being made in the likeness of God.* For GOD is not a man, even in form, although the Divine LORD is represented as assuming the human form when HE becomes manifest as ADONAI, the Divine Man, hereby signifying that man has the attributes of ADONAI, and can make ADONAI manifest through those attributes.

THE IMMANENCE OF GOD

It is a wonderful vision. When you understand it in its innermost significance you know that the FATHER-MOTHER is in HIS universe, and that HE is transcendently great and yet exquisitely beautifully immanent. When I look at the Stars, I see HIM. When I behold their motion, I know it is HIS own motion in them. I catch something of HIS majestic glory which they pour forth upon the magnetic plane. I love to see these realms from within, and to catch their glory; for to see them in their resplendence is to behold HIM in manifestation; to know that their substance is HIS own, that the sublimity of the purpose of their creation is just an exposition of HIMSELF, that HE embodies HIMSELF in them, reveals HIMSELF through them, and ministers universally by means of them. To see and know HIM thus is to know that HE is in HIS creation; and that the things in this world which are so distracting, which men and women are witnessing with fear, are not of HIM at all, except in this sense that they are caused, first by the state of the Planet, and secondly as a result of the processes, and the activities which produce the processes, of that Divine magnetic action by means of which this world is to be healed and restored, and made once more the Holy City of Jerusalem—that Holy City which is to be a delight to the Heavens and a joy to all the children who dwell upon her planes.

II

THE MYSTERY OF SOLAR MOTION

Those wheels in the vision of the Prophet express perfectly such transcendent Immanence; and the Four Living Creatures moving together, represent eternal motion of the Divine in the planes of the Divine World, the creative planes of the Divine World. They represent also the

creative planes of this world in an unfallen state. And the
conditions upon the outer planes of this world which
produce seismic phenomena which fill the heart of men
and women with fear, are the result of the play of the
magnetic forces of the Divine World upon the inner
planes of the Planet, supporting and equilibrating them,
enriching them and intensifying their action unto perfect
healing. For the day is hastening that is to witness the
perfect restoration of this world. All that is in false
position and wrong estate has to be righted.

Verily, it has been the majestic Love of the FATHER-
MOTHER in HIS ministry to the inner planes of this world,
that has prevented the world from being utterly lost.
For every motion has had to be guarded lest the inner part
of the Planetary constitution should have become as the
outer planes. Material science does not think in this way.
Its explanations rarely explain anything. We know what
science thinks about the inner part of the Earth. But then
it does not know anything for certain, it just speculates.
It knows no more of the interior of the Earth or the Sun
than it knows that which is resident within a human
body filling it with deep and Divine feeling, having its
motion even through the lifestream of the body. Physical
Science knows nothing of the spiritual man and the
spiritual woman. It has no place for the Divine Man. It
has no place for nor understanding of a Planet-Soul.
Science knows no more about the Heart of the Planet
than it does about the Divine Being within a man. This
is not said in any derogatory sense of material science so
far as it is reverent and truly seeking knowledge. But it is
condemnatory of many scientific assumptions that are
made and which we know to be incorrect, and which are
as far from the truth as the darkness is from the light.

Thus much are we constrained to say for the majesty of

the Presence of the FATHER-MOTHER in HIS creation. To see HIM in the motion of a perfect world! Ah! that is a grandeur of vision beyond telling.

Come with me for a few moments to the Sun. Let your spirit take flight with me through the Celestial realms and behold HIM in the heart of the Solar Body. We find a very different world from that which physical science has led us to expect. We behold a glorious world ensphered in a photosphere, through which great magnetic activity is expressed, and which is necessary in these days for this world and other members of the system. When we get there in our Being, we shall pass in consciousness through one of those great spots upon the photosphere, a cavity so large that it is computed it would take all the members of the Solar family within itself. When we pass within, what do we find? We meet millions of glorious Beings. Of course, we meet them on the way, long, long before we reach the Sun, for they are in motion from it and back to it again because of increasing ministries. Even since we gathered here there have been proceeding the Heavenly Hosts from out that glorious Body to accompany us. They pour out upon us of their magnetic streams. They are ever with me. And they come to be with you also in these days of your fellowship, your new hope, your re-juvenation. For these are the days of your return to the consciousness of being HIS holy children, consecrated to everything that is high and true and beautiful, to be made manifest in the life that is equipoised and polarized in HIM, the life clothed from HIM, the life whose very garments are glistening with HIS resplendence. For HE throws upon you the Garments of HIS own glory.

* * * * * *

In the innermost Solar Kingdom we see the "Four Living Creatures." They are the Four Eternities accommodated to a system like the Sun. We behold the Wheels in wonderful mysterious motion. These are the creative Planes of the Solar Body. All these are full of eyes. The Divine in them sees everywhere; for they are filled with the Omniscient consciousness of the Divine Presence. This is a macrocosmic revelation of the Mystery that finds expression in the fashion of the Soul. For when a Soul's Wheels or Planes are in perfect motion, and it has attained, then its Wheels are also full of eyes. The Being knows. The Soul is able to function within the realm of Omnisciency. It is not of and in itself omniscient; but through its equipoised yet volatile Wheels in their upward and forward motion, it can touch the realm of the Omniscient, and know, to the extent that the FATHER-MOTHER doth purpose it may know, all things.

THE HOSTS WITHIN THE SOLAR WORLD

Within His glorious world of the Sun we meet with familiar faces. There are many radiant countenances. We meet with the Hosts of the LORD, Angels and Archangels. We recognize the great ones, whom of old time we have known. We meet with Michael, Uriel, and Gabriel. We see the processes of mysterious activities which are not only creative, but which are also redemptive. We come to understand the meaning of the tremendous phenomena observable by means of the veiled telescope, and also the unseen potencies analysed by means of the spectroscope. We are shown the constitution and the purpose of the photosphere and chromosphere, and we learn that in their original estate these were the result of the magnetic action within the Sun. We are shown the inner planes. They are like a tremendous generating station—though, of course, all human terms fail to express what is meant. The intense magnetic currents which are generated are projected through the media of the various atmospheres contained within the photosphere and chromosphere of the Sun, into the atmospheres of the Earth. The Solar atmospheres were at one time part of its outer Angelic Realms. But these now form the photosphere. They had to be changed in their constitution, first to act as a guard to the Divine Heavens of the Solar World against the effect of the conditions prevailing upon the Earth, and then to become a venue for the new order of Solar ministry, which the changed conditions had made necessary. The spots in the photosphere are great windows through which the Divine World looks out upon as well as ministers unto, this world, projecting into and through the photosphere such magnetic forces as will transmute the elements required by the Earth into such conditions as will make it possible for the Earth to receive them unto its healing and nourishment.

*   *   *   *   *   *

The Sun is a most glorious world. Some day soon it may be possible to speak to you more fully and intimately of the sacred Mystery expressed in, and through the Solar embodiment. Even with such an unveiling I would have you behold the Sun as a glorious world. I would have you see how the Divine Presence is transcendently revealed within and through the Sun in the motion of the Eternities. For these contain the Four great Atmospheres and the Four great Breaths within and by means of which the Wheels move backwards and forwards performing their service before the Lord, and accomplishing by such motion, His holy, glorious Will. We live in the midst of a tremendous universe. But it is not a terrible one. Where things have become terrible in the human sense, the cause is to be found primarily in the fall of those who should have been as Gods in their regnancy; then in the betrayal of the Earth and fall of its kingdoms; and then in the continued descent of man.

* * * * * * *

This is the burden of the first aspect of this wondrous Mystery set forth in Ezekiel. I would deeply impress it upon you, even until you come into that state wherein GOD moves in you, your motion becomes always HIS motion; and your thoughts, your feelings, your desires, become the exposition of your Soul's passion; and in its motion that passion becomes the exposition of HIMSELF in HIS Passion; and thus your life grows full rounded until it is such as becomes the Sons of GOD and the inheritors of HIS Mystery, in your degree.

Even as the Sun is HIS glorious embodiment in Celestial and Divine estate, so HIS glory should fill us unto such fulness that there would be projected through our auric atmosphere, such magnetic streams as would transmute the different atmospheres found in our ministry upon the Earth. For such streams of Divine magnetic flow would change, by their influence, even the desires deep-seated in men and women, influence them to higher purpose, to nobler feeling, to diviner outlook, and win them to become sharers of the Divine Love in its Passion for the perfect healing of life in this world, and for the perfect healing of the world itself.

Oh, for that life to be realized and made manifest by the Sons of GOD that would contribute to the restoration of the Planet-Soul Judah, and all her Hierarchy, and help in the bringing back of Lucifer, the great and glorious Lucifer, to be again as he was at one time, the Angel of the Outermost Sphere who was in high estate, so that he could be once more free as the Light in his flight, and full of unfettered, holy energy, to enable him to fulfil perfectly the Divine Will in glorious ministry!

III

THE DISTINCTION GIVEN TO ISRAEL

Now for a moment or two I will speak of another aspect.

You will note the distinction given to Israel in that this Divine Message was sent very specially to the whole House of Israel. You will also recognize at once the problems that have confronted the translators and interpreters. Scholars can make nothing of those sections of the Book which are set forth in apocalyptic visions. Reverent scholars, great scholars, men who are the teachers in the theological world to-day and whose books from the standpoint of scholarship have never been excelled, honestly confess that the Book of Ezekiel (with the exception of those portions of it which seem to be so clear that a child can understand them, where they speak about sin and the responsibility of the individual) contains imagery such as cannot be understood, and that the Prophet must have meant things which he could not express; just as many poets find great difficulty in expressing their intuitions. For nature poets as well as spiritual poets find great difficulty in expressing what they are looking out upon and inwardly feeling and realizing. But if scholars cannot understand the Mystery couched in these passages how can it be imagined the House of Israel could? And if not, then what was the good of sending such a message to Israel?

Yet there must have been purpose in it. But if the message was of great value, why should it be so hidden? Why should it be largely presented as a cryptograph, or a writing that is absolutely veiled? And why should it be presented in hieroglyphs unfamiliar to the people?

Whilst the difficulty appears to be great on the surface,

it is not actually so. There was a time when Israel understood such hieroglyphs. There was a time when Israel understood the meaning of the Four Living Creatures in the degree in which the Mystery related to the Sun. For, as I have indicated elsewhere, all things have their degree of exposition and embodiment. A planet has only a degree in comparison with the many degrees of the Solar Body; and the latter has only comparatively few degrees in comparison with the Universe. But the Principle is one; the Life is one; the Light is one; the Realization is one; though the degree of the Life, the Light and the Realization, is according to the estate of the individual, whether of Soul, Planet, or Sun. Therefore in their degree the Children of Israel understood the wonderful imagery in which the prophetic Message was couched.

Why should this Message be sent unto the House of Israel? Why not also unto the House of Judah? Why were not similar messages sent unto the Egyptians, or the Samaritans, or the Assyrians, or the Edomites? Are not they all children of the FATHER-MOTHER and in some ways connected with Israelitish history? Because Israel, the real Israel, alone could understand the Message.

THE GUARDING OF DIVINE SECRETS

And the Secrets of GOD revealed unto Beloved ones must needs be guarded. They have to be protected from those who misuse them. What do you think would happen to-day in the realms of material science, where great minds are ever seeking to discover the secrets at the heart of the universe, if they were successful? What do you think might happen if such things could be revealed to those who do not relate them to the All-Presence of the FATHER-MOTHER? Why, they would destroy the world, even as in past ages they brought about many calamities and put

back for great cycles the healing of the planes of this dis-
traught world. These Secrets must be approached reverently. Men must learn to handle them as Divine Sons
rather than as great minds. Those to whom these Secrets
have been unveiled may not discover them to the
Nephelim in the world who are ever seeking power
through knowledge for individual, communal, national,
and racial ends.

Because of this the very elements in which Divine consciousness is inherent, have to be guarded; for they are of
the Divine Ætheria out from the bosom of which all
things have become. For the Divine Ætheria is the substance out of which all things are upbuilt. Of it is begotten
the motion of the Eternities named the "Four Living
Ones," through which the Four Breaths blow. When the
Four Breaths move through the Divine Ætheria, it is then
gathered and formulated into Systems, Stars, Planets, and
the lesser individual Sons of GOD, named in their first
Celestial estate, Human Souls. What think you might
happen even in this world in relation to the generation of
Human Souls and their growth as they proceeded along
the path of their Divine evolution, and as they took their
ascending arcs by which they passed from degree to
degree and attained to Divine consciousness, if the
Secrets were discovered by material science which are
hidden in the heart of the Divine Spiral in every man and
woman, and the Divine Substance out of which the Spiral
was fashioned, and the Spiral itself whose very function is
the result of the play of the Four Breaths through the
Divine Ætheria or Divine Substance out of which the
Being was built up into consciousness, and the Soul's
planes which are all attached to that Spiral, and the Four
Creative Ones named the Living Creatures whose motion
upon the four lower planes is for the calling forth into

manifestation of the Soul's attributes? The Human Races might be destroyed.

But GOD has guarded HIS Secrets, and man cannot know them by any knowledge wrested from the elements of nature or gathered from without. No one who knows those Secrets can unveil them even to another; for he must needs speak of them in language which in itself veils them. Those who would know the Divine Secrets must come by that path which is the only royal road into that estate of consciousness wherein the Divine World itself may become unveiled. And because the House of Israel had come along that road, as its goal related to the Solar Body, the cryptographic Message came to them. It was unto them that this marvellous vision of the Spiral came with its whirlwind of Divine motion and the sacred Flame rushing through it and making the whole Spiral become in form like the Divine Man; and which at the base became as a throne of sapphire, called a Chariot of Fire, that moved upward and downward enveloping all the Being like a cloud of pure amber glowing with the indescribable radiance of the Flame, the motion of the Flame causing the manifestation of the Radiance.

Israel had learnt the Secret to a large extent of the superstructure of the children of men upon the planes of this world. Nay more. They understood the architecture of the Planet. Though many Secrets still remained veiled from them, yet they had learnt many things according to their degree of reverence attained through upward flight and Godward motion, and according to the intensity of the motion of the Eternities within them expressed through the Living Wheels full of eyes, and the ascending and descending of the Flame in their Spiral as this latter responded to the Eternities and expressed the Spirit's motion in the four dimensional estates—the Human, the

Angelic, the Celestial, and the Divine; estates or kingdoms which were all within them.

Think of the distinction given to Israel that these Mysteries should be sent to them; that they should have such a revelation of the majesty of the FATHER-MOTHER through HIS Christ to recall to their remembrance what once they knew when they were dwellers elsewhere than upon this Planet! Think of the distinction given to them from amidst the vast multitudes of GOD's children upon the planes of this world, and the reason that such Mysteries could be sent to them in cryptograph and cryptogram, because they were the only children upon the Earth who could receive them, even in lowly degree! Think of it that Ezekiel, a Prophet thought to have been a Priest in the Jewish temple, which, of course, was impossible because of its creature sacrifices, but who was a Priest of the Most High GOD, a Seer in transcendent vision, could receive from the Innermost Realm the majestic representation of the most sacred Mysteries to present in hieroglyph unto the Children of Israel! Think how the Divine Love unto this day has guarded the Revelation by its very terms! And now the interpretation is coming. Now you may see the story of the constitution of the Soul, the constitution of the Planet, the constitution of the Sun, and even of the Universe, hidden in the Book; together with the great betrayal, the Redemption, and the Regeneration.

Oh, how profound are the ways of our FATHER-MOTHER! How deep beyond human mind understanding! Yet the Soul who knows HIM can understand them. At the very feet of Israel, in these days of the Return, a wealth of sacred story from the very Table of the LORD of Life is laid, in the hope that Israel shall awaken and remember, and in the remembrance re-discover all that

they were; all that once they knew of the glory of their
FATHER-MOTHER; the splendour of their setting forth
from that happy, transcendent, Celestial Home of the
Celestial Christhood, to come here to be HIS Mediators,
Seers, and Interpreting Prophets. Many of them came to
lay aside even those high offices and become the teachers
of the little spiritual children upon the Earth, interpreting
to them through the language of the flowers, the exceeding
grace and beauty of the fashion of the FATHER-MOTHER
Who is in every perfect form, and Who reveals HIMSELF
in all things that are true and beautiful and equipoised,
and that are magnetically so conditioned that their manifestation and their motion are contributory to the enrichment of life and the spiritual wealth of the world, adding
to the beauty of the world, to the glory of GOD made
manifest from the heights into the depths, revealing HIS
Love and Wisdom in the world's greatness as a system
before HIM, and the world's humblest exposition of HIS
energy in it and through it, in the little flower. For even
the spiritual child-man can look on and admire and study
and learn after his degree.

O beloved ones of the FATHER-MOTHER! Behold the
distinction with which HE regards you! HE has preserved
those Secrets in that strange book of cryptograph and
cryptogram that Israel may behold in this day something
of HIS own Mystery as the writings are recovered and their
meanings unveiled. And although the fulness of meaning
found in the language may be as yet beyond you, still, if
you will read reverently, humbly, prayerfully, with the
Divine intent only to be more perfectly HIS own, all that
the vision speaks of will become clear to you, and you will
behold HIM ever more fully as the most glorious ONE, the
path of Whose Love is in the great Deeps, and the realm
of Whose glory is revealed everywhere in HIS Wisdom.

What further HE would have Israel know will be spoken of bye and bye.

Ever Blessed be HIS glorious Name! Oh give thanks unto HIM always. Give praise to HIM continually. Live in the consciousness of HIM. If you do so in the measure in which you are able, then, though the shadows steal towards your threshold, HE will enable you to turn your countenance away from the shadows. HIS radiance through you will chase them away, even though sorrow may still seem to sit upon your brow and cause its lines to be shadowed forth in your face. Israel must not seek to be relieved from all burden-bearing, but to learn how to share the Divine Sorrow in and for the world. Yet, if you turn your countenance to HIM so that you will remember again that HE is with you, that HE is in you, that you dwell with HIM, even the outlining of the sorrow will pass; and HE will fill you with HIS glory and transform you unto the outermost and transfigure you within until you are clothed with the Light of HIS own glorious radiance. I would have you lovely in all your thoughts and consciousness of HIM. You are becoming so more and more; I would yet hasten this realization within your consciousness, until you know HIM even as once HE was known by you.

O my Father-Mother! How wondrous is Thy way, even in this day of the world's travail, that Thou shouldst have found so many of Thy children, and that they should have heard Thy call and set their faces towards Thy Orient to begin their pilgrimage home to Thee, evermore to dwell in the consciousness of Thee.

May this hour be to each one Thy Holy Eucharist in them and the most Sacred Mass of their Being's offering unto Thee!

And may they all be encompassed by Thy Heavenly Hosts and overshadowed by the Radiant Cloud, that all may behold Thy Glory, and evermore Praise and Serve Thee! Amen and Amen.

THE MESSAGE OF EZEKIEL

A COSMIC DRAMA

★

Part Four (contd.)
B

★

A TRANSCENDENT VISION (contd.)—
THE DISTINCTION GIVEN TO ISRAEL

IV (contd.)
THE DISTINCTION GIVEN TO ISRAEL

You will remember that in the first unveiling I spoke to
you of the apparently strange nature of the composition
of the Book of Ezekiel, and the hieroglyphic language in
which it had been written. Most of the Book is cryptographic. It contains a hidden message that has to be
read as a cypher by one who is acquainted with the signs
and terms. The outstanding thought in the opening
vision is of the Transcendency of GOD the FATHER-
MOTHER, revealed in the resplendent vision of the motion
of the Planes and Kingdoms of the Inner Realms, with
their corresponding motion in the Planetary constitution
in its unfallen days, and also with a microcosmic correspondence in the Human Soul.

All things which a child of the FATHER-MOTHER is
capable of attaining unto must be written on the walls of
its Being. Indeed they must have been hidden by HIM
in the Divine Principle of its Life. And the discovery
and entering into the vision of these, with the ultimate
realization of the meaning of the most glorious Mysteries,
indicate the process of the unfolding of the Life itself as it
grows up and proceeds through the ages, evoluting and
evolving from degree to degree within each Kingdom
until it arrives at that estate wherein it can celebrate its
jubilee and sing its jubilate or song of triumph and attainment. For the ultimate of the Soul in its growth and
ascension is to attain this high estate wherein it can live
evermore in the consciousness of the Omniscient and
Omnipotent ONE, and be continually touched from HIS
realms, so living as to have all the Being's motion in HIM
and from HIM, and consequently for HIM.

You will also remember how I drew your attention

to the outstanding fact, which is most evident in the Book, of the great distinction conferred upon Israel as a people and a nation. As a race of the Sons of GOD they were singled out to be the recipients of that cryptographic writing, in order that in the days to come, which were then anticipated and concerning which many things were prophesied and projected, wherein they would realize a reascension of consciousness and a resurrection of all their attributes and powers, they might come into the understanding of their Ancient Heritage, couched in the transcendent vision as it related to the superstructure and inner motion of their own individual Being.

This morning I take you to the other aspects to consider them. I will just repeat the five I repeated then:—

1. The Transcendency of GOD,
2. The Mystery behind the motion of the Four Living Ones and the Wheels full of eyes,
3. The distinction of Israel,
4. The resurrection or restoration of Israel,
5. The rebuilding of the Temple, with the restitution of the Priesthood.

In opening this second portion of the unveiling, I have to return to the third aspect; that is, The Distinction conferred upon Israel by the Great Love.

In the Book as it stands, Israel is GOD's elect people; but they are HIS elect people from out the midst of the land of Judah. And they are chosen quite irrespective of their estate, of their past heritage, of their splendid attributes, of the ministries they may have rendered through the ages. According to the statement, they are simply elected at GOD's pleasure.

Those of you who have been trained in the Scottish or Nonconformist communities where ultra Calvinism has been taught, will recognize the calamitous introduction of such a thought into this Book. It shows the hand of the betraying scribe. For here, as in other parts of the Book, there are manifold evidences of the hand of the representative of the two religions of Israel. This will be emphasized when I come to speak of the Temple. Pre-destination is clearly set forth, as that was interpreted by John Calvin, and even more so by many of his followers. But though Israel is chosen to be the "Peculiar People of GOD" in the midst of the land of Judah, the Prophet is counselled to proclaim their individual responsibility. The honour conferred upon them is also thus represented, that they are chosen by the Eternal to be the Shepherds of Judah in the midst of the land. They are also oft-times spoken of as the Shepherds of Israel, and an appeal-ing form of address is frequently made unto them— "O Shepherds of Israel."

In this section the doctrine of grace is also set forth as, possibly, that doctrine was theologically conceived of by Calvin, wherein the children of Israel, irrespective of their qualities, their goodness, their love, their attributes, their ministries, their devotion to GOD, are made the children of grace, the children upon whom the Divine favour falls, whilst the most terrible judgments are uttered against such lands as Assyria, Edom, and Samaria, and their inhabitants.

THE HAND OF THE BETRAYERS

Here we see something of the hand of the betrayers. Israel as a community of the Sons of GOD, though they have had the highest possible Message sent to them from the Inner Heavens, are quite lost. The glorious Heritage which Israel possessed is spoken of as if it were solely composed of the plains, the valleys, the pasture lands and the hills of Palestine.

The Book is thus most mixed in this relationship and we have to discover the hidden gems. And when we discover them and bring them out of their false settings and unveil them, they refract and flash the glory of GOD, revealing something of HIS own resplendence as that is always beheld by the Seer and communicated unto him as Revelation unto GOD's children. All revelations of the FATHER-MOTHER unto HIS children are resplendent. Even if HE is said to chide them, there is in such chiding the motion of HIS own glorious Passion of Love. It is not chiding in the sense of blaming. There is no attitude of blame in the heart of GOD. Do you account human love as perfect that is in an attitude of blame? Oh no! A human Soul being yet far from perfect may not understand. But perfect Love understands. Blame could have no place in it. It would understand the situation. It might grieve. Oh yes! It would grieve that it had to chide. Yet its chiding is not blame: it is sweet and beautiful. It is of the very character of Love itself. Perfect human love is Divine Love expressed through the human avenue. And all revelations of the FATHER-MOTHER are full of the resplendence of HIS own glory. Thus you may always know when a Message is from HIM, and when the scribe has accommodated it to his national, racial, and religious feeling, outlook, judgment, desire and purpose.

DUALISM IN THE JEWISH SCRIPTURES

In the religious history and revelation portrayed in the Old Testament, there are two distinct views of GOD in the Religion of Israel. There is the GOD Who is always rebuking, condemning, or threatening, and then suddenly professing to be compassionate. HE is not unlike Ahriman. Even a perfect man, notwithstanding the smallness of his spiritual estate in comparison with the

Eternal Mystery, and whose human vision would be limited, would be more beautiful and equipoised. But GOD is not a man, nor like some earthly potentate who is ever seeking to get his own way, and who threatens his people, compelling them into obedience by powers that inflict pain upon them if they will not render obedience.

But there is also the GOD of most transcendent Love and Wisdom—the Eternal Love, Life and Light. HE is the GOD of the true Seer and Prophet. It is HE who unveils HIMSELF within the Sanctuary and Who projects and works unto the accomplishment of the deliverance, redemption and restoration of Israel.

The laws of GOD are operative everywhere. HE need not blame nor condemn. HE need not in an individual or world sense, like an earthly judge, sit in judgment. HIS laws in their outworking bring the results to the wrong-doer. No one can do wrong without feeling the operation of HIS law. It becomes manifest through them. HIS laws are perfect, bending back or turning the Soul. In the XIX Psalm it is said, "The Law of the LORD is perfect, converting the Soul." That is, the operation of the Law causes it to return. The operation of the Law of GOD is the revealing to the Soul of its wrong doing. That is the influence which causes it to turn back from its wrong thoughts and ways. GOD's law is perfect. And no Soul has perfect comfort within itself until it is conscious that it is obeying the highest and truest and best within itself. That is the Law of GOD operating in the degree in which that Soul can cognize the Law of GOD, and the operation of the Presence within itself.

THE ANCIENT SONS OF GOD

Then we come to other parts in the Book where Israel is most manifestly presented as the Ancient People of GOD.

They are Souls who were in high estate, and who had been sent as Shepherds to this world to be guides, teachers, and interpreters unto its elder children.

The Sons of GOD and the ancient Children of Israel were one race. They were those who came to compose the communities known as Ancient Israel. And they were quite distinct from the Jewish nation that took the name of Israel. These latter were the children of Judah. The Sons of GOD had realized high estate within themselves. When they were sent out from their own System they brought with them Angelic and Celestial knowledges. They knew the meaning of many of the Mysteries of the Kingdom. And in relation to these, it was not simply knowledge about the Mysteries, but those knowledges which were the resultant of their own realizations.

It was they who laid the foundations of all spiritual science, and of all true art and music. They were the interpreters. They gave the language by which the Vegetable Kingdom could be rightly interpreted. Concerning the flowers, they revealed the meaning of their form, their colour, their economy in the earth's life, and, in so far as the Elders knew the secret of the spirit in them, they taught the most advanced Souls the Mystery. In so far as the children of the Adoption (the eldest of the children of Judah—the Planet) could receive that teaching, they interpreted to them the sublime mystery of the spirit in the trees, plants, flowers and fruits. Those who were taught by the Elders of Israel in their turn rendered service to those in lower estate. And thus from degree to degree, progressed the spiritual education of the race. There were the various orders of ministry, with none greater and none less but all ministrants for the FATHER-MOTHER; some greater than others in the degree of their realizations and, consequently, able to teach the more inward meanings of the Mysteries; others having had such communicated to them, were able to serve and re-interpret them. It was like the Bread broken and re-broken, and then again re-broken, according to the needs of those who were taught.

Here then is revealed something of the real meaning of the distinction that was conferred upon Israel. Israel has been in this world for thousands of ages. They are the Souls who never feel at home upon this Earth. And they would feel this even if the world were redeemed back to primal glory and again perfected in all its planes. They are Souls with unutterable Divine longings. In their innermost Being they love the trek Homeward. In these days this is most obviously manifest in returning Israel. They rejoice in a measure of spiritual life and Divine revealing, such as they have not had for thousands of ages since the great Descent was fully accomplished, which has come to them through the Message. In that Descent they became involved through their love for those whom they taught. They were the Shepherds. The Shepherd who seeth the wolf coming and fleeth to save himself, leaving his sheep to the enemy, is no true shepherd. He is unworthy of his office. Therefore, the Children of Israel as the Sons of GOD were the real and true Shepherds. They saw the wolf approaching in the changed conditions, but they did not flee from them. They did not seek to save themselves. They did not take the wings of the spirit and fly from their service. No, they said amongst themselves, "We will strive against these new and foreign forces; we will continue our service; we will persist in our ministries; we will try to overcome all the hurtful conditions."

HOW ISRAEL ARE DISCOVERED

But there came the day when the changes became

so tremendous in the Planetary constitution, and they found themselves so very heavily involved, that they lost the vision of their past. They forgot. And so they lost the memory of HIS countenance Who was their LORD. They even forgot the names and the Message of the Messengers who had been sent unto them. They forgot the Messenger who was most frequently with them, though they were his spiritual children, those whom the FATHER-MOTHER had given unto him. Being drawn down by the depressing, materialistic and occult conditions, they became so involved in the states of the Planetary life that they lost their communal and regal distinctiveness. *Then took place the real diaspora.* They were scattered. From time to time they were taken up again out of the depths of soul-despair into which they had gone down. That was work for the Angels and the Messenger. They were known through the burning of the Sacred Flame within their Lamp. That most Sacred Flame has always had its motion Godward, even though the radiance became veiled. It is the Flame in their Lamp which was lit great ages ago from the LORD. It does not mean that other Souls have not that Flame. Every Soul has it potentially. Many have that Flame in very small degree. But Israel had it in large degree. When spiritual influences came from the Angelic World and affected Israel, that Flame came up again. As the Heavens have been able to Overshadow them, the Flame has more and more become manifest.

Now you will understand how the Angels of GOD in their ministry to-day are to find Israel. They know them by this Flame. *He knoweth them that are His.* HE knoweth those who were old enough in their spiritual growth and evolution to have the Flame of the Spirit burning in such a degree within them; for the spiritual resultant of the

Overshadowing is to make the Flame burn sufficiently strongly to be seen from the Inner Worlds. Nay more. When the Flame burns intensely, there ascends from it as from the censer the golden incense of the Soul's emotion. The incense is the atmosphere of prayer. Real prayer is the Soul's emotion moved to the Deeps, Godward. It is not simply the utterance of words; rather is it the inarticulate cry of the Soul. The loveliest prayers are beyond articulation in human speech. Those of you who love music turn from human speech which you find inadequate, and endeavour to express through the organ or other instrument something of the intonation of your Being; but you cannot through any instrument or in any tongue articulate the deepest, which is also the highest, yearning of your Being for the FATHER-MOTHER. Thus, when that Flame is in motion, there is beheld the inarticulate language of the golden incense ascending to the Heavens.

IV

THE RESTORATION OF ISRAEL

The distinction given to the Sons of GOD was such as to crown them with a consciousness of the Divine Love and Wisdom, and a fulness of remembrance of fellowship in the Inner Realms, so that, whilst dwelling upon these planes, they were able to think backward through the ages. And they were able to let their Flame rise up into the Heavens, sending the incense of their prayers as the golden incense of Divine Love, to bring back in increasing fulness the outpouring from the Angelic Realms, and even the Divine Realms.

Therefore, when Israel had to be found, the Angels had to find them. The Angel of the LORD had to find such in the midst of Israel as could respond to this Message wherein is HIS own revealing. HE had to send HIS

Messenger at times to reveal once more unto Israel their own ancient history, their Soul Heritage, their relation to the Inner Worlds, and their relation to this world as His Shepherds in Judah.

And what a distinction it was! To be called of God to reveal His grace! For grace is the beauty of Love. It is the radiance of Love. It is the motion of Love within the Being that makes it gracious in all its action and in all its manifestation. For no one can be full of Divine Love without being gracious. *To realize the Divine Love is to become sons and daughters of grace.* And that does not mean mere favourites of the Heavens. What it does mean is this, that children of grace are revealers and manifestors of the favour or grace of the Heavens. That makes life a reality. To be a son of grace is to be a revealer and manifestor of the graciousness of the Love of God, the tenderness of that Love, the beauty of that Love in its deportment to others expressed in the motion of the life through every act and every word. *The favour of God unto His People is the revealing of Himself as they are able to receive. In this way He communicates Himself.*

Israel had received greatly; otherwise they would never have been sent here to be the Shepherds, Teachers, Interpreters, real Scientists, Artists, Revealers in the world; the interpreters of God in nature, in planetary and stellar motion; the interpreters of God in the superstructure of Life and of the Soul itself. The Greater Mysteries concerning these things could only be unveiled even in those far-away unfallen days, to the few; for the Soul has to grow from the realm of manifestation in the without, until it comes to the realm of manifestation in the within, which is the realm of the great realization.

Now you will understand the meaning of that marvellous description of the Restoration of Israel. It is thought of in theological circles to be a prophecy concerning the resurrection of the body from the grave. It is taken as testimony in the Old Scriptures of the actual resurrection from the earthly grave of the bodies of all Souls who passed over. There are those who still believe that the body rests in the grave until the resurrection day. The Scottish Catechism affirms this. So do the Episcopal and Roman Churches in their Articles.

Here again may be observed the hand of the enemy fixing the children's thoughts upon the material aspect of the great spiritual truth. When a boy, the statement in the Shorter Catechism arrested me, which says—"The souls of believers are at their death made perfect in holiness, and do immediately pass into glory; their bodies meanwhile resting in the grave until the resurrection." Naturally the child enquired, Why it was necessary for such Souls to come back to get earth-bodies, if they were made perfect and enjoyed the glory of the Ever Blessed ONE. But though he asked the question, the Elders were silent, or they silenced the child. No light shone in their spiritual system.

A MIRACULOUS EVENT

The picture portrayed in the prophecy is cryptographic. It is even presented from the human aspect as if it were the resurrection of the body in all its parts, bone coming to bone, sinew to bone and sinew, building up into their several relationships the different parts of the body, with the flesh covering the ligaments and sinews, and then the flesh covered by the skin—which is necessary as a defence and which has a mystical signification of GOD putting HIS defence about you.

It is a wonderful vision, individual and communal, of the restoration of Israel's planes and vehicles to that Life in HIM which is begotten of the consciousness of HIS ensphering and overshadowing. It is the bringing back to Israel, whose memory had been veiled through the ages, and whose manifestation had ceased to express the fulness of the Christhood, of that Life which was once realized by every member of the Christhood community. It signified the bringing back again of the whole Household of Israel to take their part once more, individually and collectively, in that transcendent motion of the four Dimensions, the four Divine Elemental Kingdoms in their ministry unto the Planet unto the equilibrating of its motion when its planes will be released once more and be able to perform their ministry before the LORD in obedience to the motion of HIS Spirit.

Thus it will be seen that the resurrection of Israel is not in any sense the resurrection of their outer bodies from graves where death reigns. Had it been so, what a number of bodies there would have been to be resurrected. For all Israel had lived thousands of times on these planes. Many find it difficult to believe they have lived here before, though now and again they are confronted with the fact in the awakening of strange memories of places and faces. And they say, "Why! I seem to recognize this one and that one; and yet I know I have not seen them before in this life." They visit a place far afield, and it awakens in them strange homelike feelings; or they are moved in most strange ways, often to sorrow for which they cannot account. Some meet in the way others they have not known in this life, and within an hour they seem to have known them all through their life; whilst others awaken antagonisms. They are *revived memorabilia*, although the individuals are not able to relate and correlate them. Yet these are the beginnings of the return to high consciousness of the Soul, and the reopening of its memory.

In the prophetic vision Israel was as a valley of slain. The Earth powers, astral and occult, had slain them. The thief in the night, represented by these powers, had taken from them their Divine Potencies in great measure, and so drained them of spiritual vitality that they forgot who they were and what they had been. They were as dead. And the prophet is shown them lying in a valley containing the remains of the dead, and is asked the question if he thinks they can ever be restored to life again. It is recorded in the opening of the Apocalypse that even the Master, of whose visions the Apocalypse is a part record, said—"*And I wondered much whether these things could again be, because of all that I saw.*" He wondered if the Seven Churches of Asia, the ministrants of GOD in this world, could ever be restored and their beautiful ministries revived. And thus also the Prophet said concerning the House of Israel—"*How should I know? Thou alone, Lord, knowest whether they are beyond recall.*"

But surely that could not be!

Then he heard the Voice saying—"*Command the Breaths to blow!*" And there followed the motion of the fourfold dimensional Life from the Eternal World.

THE ARISING OF ISRAEL

The vision of the Valley of dry bones is related to the opening vision, for its hidden meaning is to be found there. The rehabilitation of Israel is the restoration of all the members of the community; the salving of them individually in all their parts; the enhancing of all their attributes and their vehicles through the healing of them, and thus bringing all their planes into perfect motion, so that they become in unity once more. And so great is the healing vouchsafed unto them through the ministries of the Four Breaths as these Breaths are wafted from the

Four Eternities, that every part is recovered and restored so as at last to be able to stand upright. And standing upright means that the righteousness and equity of GOD are restored in them, even the equilibrium of the Cross. They are once more upright and in balance. They stand upon their feet, and have again the understanding of the Divine Secrets. They stand upon the foundation of Truth. They stand upon their feet made beautiful in all the ways of Life. They stand upright with all their attributes and vehicles so equilibrated that these can be marshalled and called into individual service; and each member being able so to stand upright, can respond to that marshalling of the whole community which makes of the whole Household of Israel no longer simply a nation upon the earth, nor a peculiar race upon the earth, nor a scattered religious people upon the earth, but none other than the Ancient Sons of GOD gathered out of Judah's conditions, reclothed with the majesty of a life made glorious as a Son of GOD, a race of Divine Souls able to take their place once more amidst the motion of the Divine World in its Overshadowing of Judah. For a restored Israel will have joy in responding to the motion of the Wheels and the Divine planes, sharing in the Breaths that blow through the Four great Atmospheres from out of the Four Dimensions or Eternities. For Israel so restored will be able once more to endure the vibrations that play upon them and within them from the Divine World.

Here is a vision of no weaklings, but of men and women fully restored to a life that is full of light and power, light that reflects and reveals the glory of the FATHER-MOTHER, and power to demonstrate HIS Presence in the life, and through the life into all the ministries of the daily service. It is a vision of the resurrection of the Sons of GOD in this

world out of the night of the Planetary conditions, out of
the valley of spiritual death which overtook the world
ages ago, and which those noble sons and daughters of the
Heavens had to share with the children of this world;
remaining with them to help them. But in order that their
own Lamps should not go out, they were taken from time
to time, in sections up on to the Bethlehem whilst the
Bethlehem remained; and when it came down in the fall
of the second magnetic plane, they were taken into the
Lower Angelic World and there nourished until they could
be sent back again. For it was necessary that their
Flame should continue to burn, and that they could be
readily found when "the fulness of time" had come and
His holy purpose had been outwrought by means of the
Oblation. For then the time of their arising would have
come when they could be found and regathered.

That time has come. It is manifest in the arising of
Souls. It is the meaning of one and two here and there
arising. The Angelic World knows them through the
Flame. The Angels have but to breathe upon the Soul,
and its Flame reveals its Heritage.

THE PROPHET NOT UNDERSTOOD

Verily the distinction and honour conferred upon Israel,
is beyond all language to portray, to measure, and to
reveal.

You will therefore understand your relationship to that
early vision. You will understand your relation to the
transcendency of the Eternal Mystery of the FATHER-
MOTHER. You will understand how it came to pass that
the Prophet named Ezekiel, as the Soul who was illumined,
had given to him such sacred Mysteries to present in
cryptographic form rather than in plain statement, so that
they should be hidden from the hands of those who

destroyed the Mysteries in other ages when these were sent from the Heavens. You will understand how it comes to pass that the Book of Ezekiel, though placed in the Canon, is the least understood of all the books in the Old Testament. You will understand that, though it has not been understood unto this day, it was the Divine magnetic hidden power in the very cryptographic presentation of the Mysteries which made the Jews hold on to it, although they questioned whether it could be in their Canon, especially because of its description of the Temple which was out of harmony with theirs concerning the Temple and its sacrifices; and likewise by the various œcumenical councils during the history of the Canon of Scripture in the Christian Church, how it has often been contended that there is conflict in it between the Jewish and Messianic ideas, and the Christian Church has considered seriously through the ages whether the book should be accounted inspired and authoritative. For the Church has felt like this notwithstanding that the Book is full of the very resplendence of the FATHER-MOTHER, though it is quite true there are many parts in the Book where HE does seem to be totally eclipsed.

THE RESTORED TEMPLE MINISTRIES

The restoration of Israel as a community of the ancient Christs to take once more their place and share in the Divine ministry unto the Planetary Redemption, eventuates in the rebuilding of the Temple. The description of the Temple given by the Prophet is entirely spiritual. It is clearly indicated that it is such; although here and there there has been introduced by some scribe, details of the sacrificial customs which obtained for great ages in Jewry. The Ancient Wisdom used the terms which came to be associated with the creatures; but the Ancient Wisdom used those terms solely to express great and profound and most holy things. The terms were cryptogrammatic. The sacrifices of the Temple, beginning with the burnt offering in the outer court, and passing on to the oblation signified by the goat offered on the Great Day of Atonement, and even unto the laying of the lamb on the altar of oblation called the Mercy Seat, represented the processional of the Soul from its own outer court to its innermost Sanctuary; the path by which it reached the innermost; a path of sacrifice full of sacred acts; a path wherein the body had to be consecrated with all its powers represented by the ox for the man and the heifer for the woman, where life in its majestic expression of the Divine Love had to be laid on the Altar as a sacrifice to be energized from the Heavens, the energizing force being called the Fire and the sacrifice the Ram. For the Ram is of Ramah which is the Divine Kingdom, and in man is Ra's sacrifice of the Life-principle unto the service of the FATHER-MOTHER.

Thus in the whole Divine order of sacrifice there is set forth the path of the Soul's processional, passing into the innermost, and attaining unto that estate wherein it acquires the power to make of itself a perfect oblation, giving everything, even to the yielding up of its will as signified by the goat, without the sacrifice of which there could be no Atonement, or an estate of Life in perfect unity between the innermost of the Being and the Divine World. The Atonement is the attaining of Divine unity in oneself, and the becoming of our whole Being one with the LORD.

As the natural corollary of that sublime attainment there is the offering of the Lamb of GOD in us, the Divine Love Principle and Arche in the Being, in absolute fulness, to be used by the FATHER-MOTHER as HE purposes, and not simply according to the Soul's choice. Some people will make a sacrifice if it can be offered in the degree and way they want. But that is not the way to the great Realization. If you make sacrifice in that way you will have to learn again from HIM that your sacrifice must be offered to HIM unconditionally to be used as HE thinks best. The perfect way is to commit everything into HIS keeping, to seek oneness with HIS motion, rise to adore within the realm of HIS glory so that HE may be able to make use of that which you offer to HIM for service. The offering up of the Soul upon the Mercy Seat, is the giving of one's whole Being to be just what the Divine Love purposes. And if the Divine Love says to such an one— *Now you have attained to a glorious estate of consciousness, and you have entered into the fellowship of the Innermost Realms, you have become one with the Gods; henceforth you are crowned a Son of God. And now it is the Will of the Heavens you should descend to a certain world that needs very special ministry which the Father-Mother asks you to render.* Such a Soul, having attained to so high an estate, would at once say, *O my Father-Mother, be it even as Thou willest.*

The Soul could not stay up there if it were unwilling to consecrate itself fully and give of itself absolutely. It is in this way that Souls acquire the power from the FATHER-MOTHER to lay down their life and to take it up again. For such divestment is not to be associated only with the Oblation. Divestment for the purpose of ministry applies to all who have attained.

V

THE COSMIC TEMPLE

In the Prophet's vision there arises a mystical Temple of which he gives a description. The Temple has a Mystery embodied in it which is veiled from the reader. Its measurement is described in mystical numbers. These relate to the building of the walls and courts. The Prophet emphasizes under strange terms the right angle and the four right angles; they are called corners. Therefore the meaning is quite hidden. Within each court there are four courts at the corners, and all those courts have corners of their own. The Prophet's description deals with geometrical formation wherein there is an unveiling of the sacred mystery of the upbuilding of the life of the individual Soul into a Temple of Life.

It is related to the cosmic Life of the glorious Ancient Christhood, and to the restoration of it upon the Earth. Geometry is a Divine Science, just as Art and Music are Divine Sciences. The world is numerically balanced and geometrically fashioned. Every system is, in an abstract yet most real way, "weighed in the balances," long before the Suns and Planets appear for ministry in the spheres of manifestation. Great is the Universe of our FATHER-MOTHER, and great is HIS Mystery in every member. Great is HIS Universe, and it is glorious in its magnificence of perfect formation and perfect balance. It is only when a disaster happens such as befell this Earth through mistaken counsel originating in a betrayal, that the balance is disturbed. And here I might just say in passing that, when the balance is greatly disturbed, the member has to go outside a certain radius; for it cannot in such a state remain in its original position in the Celestial realms. Thus a whole system may be affected.

Here, those of you who think deeply along certain lines, will see a meaning in what many scientists have supposed to be the case concerning the Sun and its system; *viz.*, that it is somehow solitary or apart from the other systems. For Sol had to make the sacrifice in order to save the Planetary constitution and Hierarchy, and all the children unto whom he ministered. That is one of the

Great Mysteries associated with the history of this system. You will see great meaning in even such a brief statement. And also in this, that the Sun is hastening back in the measure in which the world is being healed. The Earth itself is not only in the intermediary ·arc, but in the measure in which it responds to the Divine ministry, the Sun is able to return. Scientists do not know where the Sun is going to. Sometimes they think he is moving around a centre. At one time it was thought to be the constellation Boötes, at another time Hercules or Alpha Lyra. But this is a secret of the Great Love, even as is the knowledge of the system to which Sol himself belongs. But in his motion he is returning with his family; and the more we can hasten on the Redemption of the children and land of Judah, the more quickly will Sol be able to take all his family back into that fuller dwelling within the magnetic Lifestream that flows from the Divine Ecliptic through his own magnetic centre.

Thus are we led to the grand resultant of the rebuilding of the Temple. The result of the building of the Temple of the Christhood in the individual life, and also in the communal exposition, is to be that each one is to be a mediator once more for the Great Love. All Israel are to be clothed in the garments of Priesthood. They are again to understand how to mediate. They are to be re-appointed to the high office of Priesthood for HIM, from before the Altar as well as through it. Their mediation is to comprise interpretation through embodiment and manifestation, mediation through revelation, and mediation in the unveiling of the sacred Mysteries of the Soul and of GOD. The glory of GOD is to be seen in and through their garments of service and praise. For the rebuilding of the Temple is the coming again of the Kingdom of GOD.

The Kingdom of God is potentially within all Israel awaiting to be made manifest.

The Kingdom of God is within you.

It is His own secret.

It is His secret in motion; and is the resultant of the motion proceeding through your superstructure.

From it proceeds the fashion of His own glory.

The Kingdom of GOD made manifest becomes the Kingdom of the Heavens. The Kingdom of the Heavens is the atmosphere generated as the resultant of the motion of the Kingdom of GOD principle within you. That is so even in the Innermost World. The atmosphere of the Kingdom is generated through the motion of the Divine Elements. The atmosphere is therefore the breath, the magnetic breath flowing from the divine centre as the result of motion. There is motion everywhere, even in the Divine World; and all Life in true manifestation is the resultant of motion. GOD used to be presented in philosophy as if HE were (except in HIS action at certain times upon and through worlds), like a quiescent pool, a GOD Who was far above and beyond HIS creation, and Who was inactive. But the Eternal Good is in all HIS creation. Even in a fallen world all the good in it is HIMSELF in manifestation; and where the good has failed to become manifest, HE works unto the healing of those conditions which prevent the good from becoming manifest. HE works through HIS Human children, as well as the Angelic children who are constantly ministering unto the Human children, and also through HIS Celestial and Divine children. The Celestial children are the Gods, the embodiments for high and glorious Archangelic and Angelic ministry.

DIVINE MEDIATORIAL MINISTRY

Unto this end you are all to be restored to priesthood, to

95

take your part in the Divine mediatorial ministry. Think of the honour of it! Think what it means to be able to mediate unto this world and its children! I know some of you think it would be lovely and glorious to have high office in the Heavens. Never think that way. I counsel you, do not seek to attain high office as such. It is not the way to attain high office. Take the office the FATHER-MOTHER gives you, and fulfil it devoutly, devotedly, and nobly, even should it be of most humble position.

It is a ministry of exquisite dignity even to understand a flower and interpret it to those who do not understand it, who do not see the beauty and the glory of the FATHER-MOTHER in its form, its colour, its radiance, its motion, its breath, its purpose. That is great mediation.

To reveal through an Art which is beautiful, and make the exposition embody a thought of GOD; to reveal through rhythm of music with its sublime intonations, the very music begotten of the motion of the Heavens; these are also great mediations.

To be able to speak to a Soul concerning itself and its attributes, encouraging it in the way by unveiling to it GOD'S Mystery within itself, is likewise high mediation. If shadows are seen in the life of one, do not let the Soul know you see them. It is not the Divine way to let a Soul see that you are aware of the shadows. The Divine way is the truly effective way to administer to it, encouraging it so that its attributes hear your voice and feel the vibration of your love. Let the effect of your message to others always be—*Take courage and grow strengthened*. Thus help the Soul to understand itself and to behold something of the Divine beauty in its own form, its attributes, its best thoughts and noblest feelings and divinest purposes. Thus call forth the flower of the Son of GOD in the Soul. Assuredly this is a high form of mediation.

How few people understand a Human Soul! How limited in numbers are the men and women who rightly understand one another! And you know well that the shadows which you think you see in others may be only imaginary, shadows cast by your own deflected vision. People look for the shadows rather than the glory. I want you to get into that state of consciousness wherein, though you may see the shadows, they will not obtrude themselves in your vision.

If you were lifting someone out of a depth, bringing them up out of a spiritual coal-pit—(if you have ever been in a coal-pit you will know how dreary and how utterly without light it is hundreds of yards beneath the surface); you would not discourage them by saying all the time how dark the place is. You would say that the sun is shining up above; Come up into the light. Rest from your labours up here amidst the sunshine and the glory. Come and enjoy such beauty as there is all around.

So do ye in your ministry to the Human Soul. When you are bringing it up be sure the one sees the light that is pouring itself through you; and let the Divine radiance go out from your eyes, even into the valley of their life. Encourage them up. Never discourage a Soul. If any-one stumbles by the way, never blight the rising hope or dim vision within them. Try to heal the hurt which the stumbling has brought to them.

Encourage them to go on. Then bye and bye they will walk without stumbling. They will stand upright and be steadfast before the LORD.

Such mediation is a far greater thing than many imagine. So may you mediate as truly as before the Altar. The Altar mediation is one aspect. It relates to the innermost where there is the unveiling of the Mysteries of GOD. It relates to the realm of prayer and to the Soul's aspiration in the individual and communal life. But the Altar is also within you and relates to prayer, to your vision and sacrifice. And from that Altar I would have you go forth to mediate in every avenue of life, and make everything you do a service for the Divine. If there be anything in it that cannot be associated with the Divine, cast it out. Make all you do become beautiful. Let your actions be harmonious in every relative part, that it may be said of you that your service is done for the Divine.

Thus through your ministry you will generate the Kingdom of Heaven in the Earth. You will bring the Kingdom of Heaven to the Earth because the Kingdom of GOD in you is actively manifesting itself, keeping you up in the Heavens of Realization and holding you up whilst also letting you down here for service. And always remember that you are upheld by the power that is there. Therefore, never walk in your own strength. Pray and serve for the day to come when you will walk in the consciousness of HIM Who is all strength to you, all light, and all glory.

THE NEW MANIFESTATION

Now at the close of the prophecy it is said that the House of Israel, marshalled as the Hosts of the LORD, are to become the manifestation of GOD upon the Earth. What a distinction! O House of Israel! to hear HIS Voice calling and behold HIS vision leading into such fulness of realization that you will be able to reveal HIM on the Earth to all HIS children as they are able to receive! What an honour, to be crowned Son of GOD, Servant of the LORD, Mediator, Revealer, Manifestor, Interpreter of the Will of the FATHER-MOTHER! Come back into the remembrance of HIS great goodness to you throughout past ages and have the assurance of HIS abiding goodness to you for all the ages to come. Walk ye in the consciousness of HIM, in the Light of HIS glory. Be upright and balanced children of HIS Love and Wisdom, raised out of the valley of the shadow of death. Be once more HIS sacred vehicles for the mediation of the Divine World. Be again HIS holy chalices, individually and collectively, into which and through which HE can pour the sacred potencies of HIS most glorious Love.

*   *   *   *   *   *

O my FATHER-MOTHER! How wonderful THOU art in THY ways! How exceedingly great THY Love is unto us, exceeding all THY children could have imagined, that in this day, out of the midst of this world that has been through the ages so shadowed, THOU shouldst be calling us back again into the consciousness of the high realization of the radiance, the potency, and the glory of THY Presence!

Thy Servant doth bless THEE. His heart's cry is, Oh, that I could reveal unto THY children yet more and more beautifully and fully, the wonders of THY Love and Wisdom!

Ever Blessed be THY glorious Name in my Being, and through it for THY service; and in THY children here; and through them for the service of THEE in and unto this very needy world.

Amen and Amen.

THE MESSAGE OF EZEKIEL

A COSMIC DRAMA

*

PART FIVE

*

THE MYSTERY OF TYRE AND ZIDON

THE MYSTERY OF TYRE AND ZIDON

In the synoptic Gospels there is more than one reference to Tyre and Zidon; but there is a special reference where it is represented that the Master spake words like these:—

"Woe unto thee, Bethsaida! Woe unto thee, Capernaum! Though thou be exalted unto the Heavens, thou shalt be brought down to hell."

Of course, the Master did not say these things, but He said things containing the Mystery of their history. And it is represented that He also said:—

"It shall be more tolerable for Tyre and Sidon in the day of judgment than for thee."

And although He did not speak after that manner, in the sacred Mysteries unveiled to the intimate ones He had to speak of the real Bethsaida of Galilee, and the real Capernaum on the Galilean Lake, and the real Tyre and Zidon on the borders of the Great Sea. There were places bearing those names; but in the Mysteries unveiled by Him they were not little cities on the shores of the Lake of Genesareth, called the Sea of Galilee in the Mysteries, nor the two on the western borders of Palestine and on the shores of the Mediterranean Sea. In history along the outer planes, Tyre at one time was a great city; so also did Zidon become. The riches of the world then known were gathered into Zidon, and afterwards into Tyre. It is said ships came from all parts bringing wealth. Thus in the mystical setting forth of a great Planetary history, the terms were again used, because they were originally mystical. Indeed, many of the most sacred names of places, cities, mountains, valleys, and rivers, were originally mystical. They related to things in the then pure Astral or Elemental Realms, and the Occult Kingdom which was adjacent to the Spiritual Realm, or Angelic

Kingdom. Those terms came to the Earth by the holders of the Mysteries. These were the Sons of GOD who knew the Mysteries. Where they settled in their pilgrimage as the teachers and leaders of the children on the Earth in the unfallen days, they gave, in the degree in which the children were able to perceive, something of those most sacred Teachings. There were many, of course, that had to be held as secrets. Only in the most tentative way could these be touched upon. But even to incite the desire in the children to learn more of the Wisdom of the FATHER-MOTHER, was to help them gradually. They had given to them here a little and there a little, to help them to come into the cognition of the sacred meaning of Soul-life, Soul history, Planetary life, Planetary constitution, Planetary motion, Planetary purpose. Then as Souls grew into the knowledge spoken of as the Wisdom relating to these things, more Celestial knowledge was imparted to them.

In a marvellous passage of the Text of Ezekiel concerning Tyre and Zidon there is an amazing revelation of this world's history, and, also, of other members of the system. Many have imagined that there is no Planetary history to speak of in the Scriptures of our Bible that have been held sacred by the Western World, and for a longer period by Jewry; yet those Old Testament Scriptures contain in a veiled form, Mysteries that are not to be found elsewhere, though they are not in a form in which they can be understood. There are certain aspects of them implied in some of the other Religions. Yet these are not given with the fulness nor with such certain knowledge lying behind the revelation, as is to be found in those Old Scriptures.

THE SITUATION OF THE CITIES

Where was the city of Tyre, and that of Zidonia, where the riches of GOD were held for service, and into which the wealth of the Isles had been brought? Whence came the many Argosies of the various nations laden with wealth with which Zidon and then Tyre were enriched? The Argosies were those of the various Divine Potentates who ministered unto this world; and the notable Ancient Cities of Zidonia and Tyre formed the upper and middle realms of the Occult Kingdom in the unfallen days of this world.

The term "occult" is practically modern, in our use of it. In ancient times it was the magnetic realm. It was the land of magnetic light. Within it were the circuli through which communications were flashed from the Heavens to this world. It was the realm whence, and the venue through which, the Light penetrated unto the children who were to become the Illuminati. It was therefore the land that was enriched for the purpose of helping them in their ministry unto the children of this world. The land of Tyre, the city of Tyre, and the inhabitants of Tyre, all speak of a great period in the history of this world, long before it was borne down into the states of materialization in which we find it to-day. But it is much better to-day than it was great ages ago. And it is now gradually to regain its ancient estate, and will do so in the measure in which all that corresponds to the ancient city of Tyrus upon these planes becomes purified, exalted in state, and put to right uses in the service of our FATHER-MOTHER.

The city of Tyre was once as an Eden. There are many who have studied the occult philosophies and have been taught in such study, that occultism and mysticism are at variance. They are to-day on the earth; but not in a pure occultism. It is only the wrong influence, and the inverted states of the mind which cause atmospheres of opposition to the spiritual and the Divine to arise, and to make it appear as if a true mental concept—for the Soul gets there before it gets unto the Great Realization—was at variance with a mystical vision of the same truth. The occultist has to operate and learn through the mind. The mystic operates and apprehends through the Soul. The occult vision comes through the mind. That is the vision which was betrayed. Tyre was brought down, even unto the state of hell. Hell means a state of disorder, of darkness, through false vision. And Tyre took Zidon with it. Zidonia was the city that held the more interior knowledges. These were not only Planetary, but also Solar and Celestial. The city of Tyre was once as the Eden of GOD! But even these outer planes were then all Edenic. The ways of the children were Edenic; even the ways of the youngest. They were pure and beautiful. There was no hurt in the little Hills of GOD, any more than in the great Mountains of GOD. The Hills and the Mountains were spiritual states. The Astral Kingdom and the higher Elemental Kingdom were pure. The elements were pure. They were obedient to the law of the Divine Spirit. They were able to fulfil the Divine Will. They never seemed to be at variance with that Will. They did not move and act in any respect contrary to the Divine Will. When the Divine spake, they all responded. If it is difficult to conceive of a world like that whilst we look out upon the world to-day, yet it is possible to look through a thousand ages and see the world as once it was, when it was the glorious Emerald Isle amidst the Great Deep. For it was the Emerald Isle of this system amidst the Great Deep of the Universe of Being. For the Emerald is this Earth's tincture. At one time the Earth was lovely in its form. It was clothed with the beauty of GOD. It was ensphered in Magnetic Light. In the day in which it was made, it bore the likeness of GOD. The Cherub overshadowed it. The Cherub represents the Overshadowing

Presence. The Occult Kingdom belonged to it. Likewise did the Elemental Kingdom named the Astral. For the true Astral Kingdom contained the elements of which Stars were also built up.

THE ESTATE OF THE PRINCE OF TYRE

You can thus see that in a perfect world the Elemental Kingdoms are as sacred as the Innermost Kingdoms, because they are the outer expositions of the sacred Mystery of the FATHER-MOTHER. The true Occult World was the city of Tyre. It had many ministrants; and it had a King and also a Prince. Who was this Prince of Tyre? And what befell him? In the description in the Text he is unveiled as one in whom the very secrets of GOD were sealed up. That means he had realized the sacred Mystery of Being. He was beautiful in no mere human or earth sense, nor in the mythical sense of Greek myth in its lower or sensuous degrees. He was beautiful as Adonis. But that implies that he was in the very fashion of a Son of GOD. He was exalted in his estate. For no one in the Celestial and Divine Kingdom can be exalted except through realization of Divine Potency. And if anyone wants or seeks after exaltation except through such estate, then that one could not be other than ultimately overwhelmed. We can only realize that unto which we have grown. We can only polarize to the measure of the Divine elements we have gathered into ourselves. We can ascend in our Being only in the measure in which we are polarized and the degree in which we can respond to the Divine Overshadowing. We can rise into the Celestial and Divine Worlds in the measure only that the Presence becomes realized within us; because all possibility of endurance within us of the play of the vibrations of the various Celestial estates through which we must pass, is dependent upon the polarization of our own Being in HIM Who is our FATHER-MOTHER. In the degree in which we are so polarized are we able to stand before the vision of HIM. This is no mere clairvoyant vision such as is sometimes beheld reflected on to the magnetic plane. It is a Soul vision in which the whole Being is open to the Divine World. No one can stand in the light of that vision, in whom HE has not been realized in the degree in which that vision reveals the ETERNAL ONE. No one can approach HIS Altar and witness the Cherubic and Seraphic ministry obtaining there, and receive of that ministry, and have a share in that ministry, except by the process of the Great Realization in the Being. The vastness of a Soul is not in that which might be accounted of the nature of human greatness or stature, but in the measure of consciousness through which the Divine World itself can open its Sanctuary unto the Being, and within that one speak, and reveal, and administer.

You will, therefore, understand that for the Prince of Tyre to have been in the fashion of ADONAI, implies that he had attained to great estate, and was plenipotentiary of the FATHER-MOTHER. He had been in Eden. He had walked with GOD. He had communed with the Angels. He had drunk of the streams there. He knew the glory of the Gods. Yet he was taken down from his exalted state. He lost his Kingdom. For there were those who came to this system who did not love an altogether spiritual world. They did not so much object to it being called a spiritual world and system; but their desires and thoughts were not after the order and purpose of the FATHER-MOTHER. They endeavoured to change the volatile nature of this world and make its elements fixed. They sought to change all the fashion of the system by affecting the individual members to change their polarity and enter into a state of fixity. They sought to change the elements into such conditions as would negative their power to retain Divine Polarity and respond to the Divine Law of magnetic attraction in fulfilling the Divine Will.

Those who desired this set out on a pilgrimage of their own. They had to leave the Celestial system where they had ministered. They came to this world. But they had to approach the system through its Hierarchy. Now, there are three orders of Hierarchy set over a world like this. There are the members of the immediate Planetary Hierarchy who are the representatives of the Occult administration, or what might be named the Occult administration of this world. There are the members of the Celestial Hierarchy who administer of the Divine Will to the Hierarchies of every member of the system. And then there are the members of the Divine Hierarchy. These administer to the Solar Body of the Divine Love and Wisdom.

THE WAY OF THE BETRAYERS

Those who sought to materialize this system came to the Planetary Hierarchy. They intercepted messages sent from the Celestial Hierarchy, and also some sent from the Divine Hierarchy. In the process of interception they changed the messages that had been sent. Through such a change misdirection was given. As a result there was brought about the gradual moving away of the Earth from its Celestial estate and its place in the Divine Magnetic Lifestream. In connection with this betrayal, two are specially named—the Prince of Tyre, and Lucifer. The Prince of Tyre was the king of the Occult Realm of this world. There are Divine Potentates who administer. Those in Divine estate become Potentates. This is not to be understood in any ordinary human sense of greatness. They are Potentates in that they have realized their inherent Divinity. They are in positions of spiritual and Divine greatness for purposes of administration. And the Prince of Tyre was the prince or king of the realm we now speak of as the Occult World. This will reveal much to you who have read occult philosophies where there are indications of conflicts and titanic battles amongst the minor Gods, though there is no clear light. He was brought down from his high estate. For those who sought to betray this world did it by an approach to and then through the individual members of the Hierarchy. They ensnared some through presenting to them a vision of their own greatness, impressing upon them how important they were as Potentates for the Divine, what an exalted state theirs was, how vast their realm of government, and how stupendous their power.

This is what is referred to earlier on in the book of Ezekiel by "the image of jealousy" that was set up at the door of the Sanctuary through which the Soul passed to the High Altar. Through jealousy there grew up pride, and through pride there were generated those states which led to disaster. It was through jealousy and pride that the noble Prince of Tyre was brought down.

It is just impossible to unveil here what is given me in vision! Pride and jealousy led to arrogance. There can be no arrogance in the sight of the FATHER-MOTHER. The spirit of arrogance is quite at variance with HIS Law, with all that HE is and with all that HE expresses and reveals. It was through such pride, jealousy and arrogance, that the whole world was brought down. In the betrayal many fell. Indeed the whole Planetary Hierarchy fell. They were the immediate Occult administrators. Another glorious Being was brought down in the fall of Lucifer, one time Star of the Morning. He was the Angel of the outermost sphere of the Planet. He was once radiant with the

Light of the Eternal. But he was betrayed and taken down into the land of darkness. There his vision became veiled; his radiance passed away. In a most real and tragic sense, the motion of the Sacred Flame in him was arrested, and the Light of that most Sacred Flame within the Lamp became darkly veiled.

THE PAST EXPLAINS THE PRESENT

Such is a glimpse into the ancient history, whose waters in their resurgent motion are lapping the shores of our own life to-day; history whose motion, in the recording of it, has brought about the outer catastrophes upon the surface of the Planet, and, at the same time, imposed atmospheric and magnetic conditions upon all Souls in this world which made it difficult for most to live rightly, purely, beautifully, and joyfully, and to give expression to the Divine nobility in them, through every avenue of life. Men sought everywhere for life's fulfilment through avenues other than those which were truly spiritual. Thoughtful men and women searched for an explanation of life that never came, because the true explanation was that which alone could be given from the Inner Realms where all things are known. If ye yourselves are seeking for an explanation of your travail in these days, and wondering why you should be so burdened, the meaning is not to be found in the ordinary interpretations of life. The explanation is that your pain and your sorrow are begotten of adumbrated magnetic forces reflected into you from out the ages. For the play of such magnetic streams is like the motion of the Great Deep, at times gently lapping the shores of your life; at other times dashing upon those shores as if they would verily engulf the land of your Being.

How great has the darkness been that fell upon this world, and how greatly has the darkness prevailed through-

out the ages, even where light was supposed to dwell! For
the centres of light to-day, or the supposed centres of
light, are as yet unwilling to hear the truth concerning our
FATHER-MOTHER, the Descent of this world and all its
children, and the way the Eternal World had to take in the
expression of HIS Love and the revelation of HIS Wisdom
unto the accomplishment of this world's Healing and Redemption. That is being effected now. The Oblation,
however great may be the long shadows of its aftermath
upon the threshold, has been triumphantly accomplished.
The Redemption of this world and the restoration of
Lucifer, and the reinstatement of the Prince of Tyre, are
assured. They rejoice to see this day. I could not unveil
so much to you if they did not. The Divine World has to
guard both the Servant and the Message. We are all
guarded. In the unveiling of much of this Message there
has to be very special guarding on the part of the Heavens.

But Lucifer is rejoicing to see this day. The Prince of
Tyre is rejoiced also. For in the near future there will be
such a restoration of himself and his Kingdom as will
enable him through his restored regnancy, to help Solomon
to rebuild the Temple of the LORD, which is the Temple of
the Christhood.

THE MASONIC MYSTERY OF THE TEMPLE

In the Masonic Mysteries the Temple of Solomon stands
for the Divine Man. The Soul having realized the Presence
of ADONAI—Who is in the individuated estate "the Son of
Man," but in the Eternal Heavens "the Son of GOD" and
"the only Begotten"—becomes the Temple of the Holy
ONE. That Soul has attained to Christhood. For the
individual the attainment is the realization of Christ; for
the community it is the corporate manifestation of Christhood. That is the building of the Temple of Solomon. To

that great work the Prince of Tyre contributed. But through the fall of the Prince of Tyre many things were changed. Notwithstanding the exalted position occupied by him at one time, he became of less estate than the individual Soul who had arrived at some measure of the realization of ADONAI, the Son of Man. How beautiful these Mysteries are when you get to the heart of them, may be here seen. They are not meaningless expressions in the Old Scriptures, though presented as if they had only a historical significance.

Now, in the Masonic Mysteries of the ancient times, the Building of the Temple was a most important one. And in the modern interpretation of the story of the building of the Temple of Solomon, the Prince of Tyre plays an important part. It is said that Hiram, or Huram, the king of Tyre, played a very important part when Solomon wanted to build the temple; for he sent woods, brass, silver, and even gold and precious stones. Nay, that he even sent artificers, or those who were versed in the most cunning workmanship.

Now the word Huram is related to a Babylonian myth, and is a Divine Name. All the Potentates of the Divine Kingdom and the Celestial Realms have Divine Names; and even those who are members of the Planetary Hierarchies. Thus you have in the Hebrew Mysteries Ya-akob-El, or the House of Jacob. Ya-akob-El was the Planetary Angel. He also had a Divine name. The name represents the spiritual estate of the individual, and then the office that the individual fills. How beautiful the Mysteries of our FATHER-MOTHER are! HIS ways are perfect, even in what we might account matters of no great moment.

Now, in the story it is said that Hiram, or Huram, was so friendly to Solomon that of his own accord he desired to share in the building of the Temple which was to be named the Temple of Solomon; and that he had built other houses in his own city and land. Now the name is that of a Divine Potentate. In the name Solomon we have "the One Lord" as that One Lord is embodied in the Solar Body. The sum of all Archangelic and Elohistic motion in the Solar Body is represented in the term Solomon. The Sun is the perfect representation of the sacred Mystery. The Solar World is the Divine World of this system. There is at the heart of it a Divine World corresponding to the Divine World which is the centre of all Celestial systems. The Sun is not only a glorious Celestial body in the Celestial Heavens, but he is Divine in his estate. He is Celestial in his elements and Angelic in his administrations. He is Celestial also in the outpouring of his potencies in a very special way for Planetary purposes. Here we have the most sacred Masonic mystery that you can imagine, the Love of the FATHER-MOTHER. For the Temple of Solomon is none other than the Temple of the Lord Christ Jesus realized by a Soul; realized corporately by a community; realized universally so far as the term may be applied to one world in a planetary sense; and in the larger sense realized by a system. The Solar Body itself, being the centre, is the exposition of the Divine Mystery of the Divine Man. Thus when it is said in the sacred story, that the Seer had a vision of the Sun full of the resplendence of the Mystery of the FATHER-MOTHER; that in that vision he beheld a Presence in the Sun whose stature was the polar diameter of the Sun, and whose stretch was the equatorial diameter of the Sun; that is a vision of a Solar Christhood, every member of the Hierarchy being a part of the whole. The whóle world of the Sun is gathered up into this vision, so that the Seer beholds a Solar Christhood represented as ADONAI.

THE COSMIC TEMPLE OF CHRISTHOOD

The building of the Temple of Solomon upon the earth, and within the Holy City Ierusalem, was the rearing of the cosmic Christhood. The once Holy House to which Hiram contributed, was none other than the building up of the Planetary Household to that degree of spiritual realization wherein it could become the vehicle for the manifestation of the Divine qualities belonging to a corporate Christhood. In the upbuilding, each Soul was to attain and be a Temple of the LORD of Being. It was to grow from being a little child in stature, the stature of Jesus. From the stature of Jesus it was to rise into the stature of Christ. And then from the stature of Christ it was to ascend into the glorious stature of the LORD of Being. It was to realize the Divine Presence within the Being, to build up such a Christhood or Temple of Solomon upon this earth. Hiram was to contribute out of the Occult Kingdom, the necessary elements, the necessary knowledges into which the Soul must grow, the necessary potencies that must be mediated unto and acquired by the Soul; thus becoming one with Solomon in this glorious ministry of building the sacred edifice of the Planetary Household, a fit Temple and Sacred House unto the LORD.

Is not that the meaning of the Seer's last vision in the Apocalyptic Vision where he beheld the coming of the time when the new Jerusalem, the holy Ierusalem, would come down from the Heavens once more to the earth, and GOD would be in the midst of HIS children to dwell with them; when they would know HIM, and dwell in HIS Temple? It was HE who provided the atmosphere. From HIM proceeded the glory. HE provided all things. HE was their Temple, for in their consciousness they lived evermore in HIM.

There is much, O children of Israel! I feel moved to say to you in this hour, but may not. Yet would I appeal to you to see the Divine Vision; to know how the Fall took place, and how all falls take place, falls which are the going out from the Presence of the FATHER-MOTHER through a descending in state. And I would have you see what is meant by allowing such things as jealousy, the image of jealousy, to throw its shadow again upon the threshold of your life, even to stand inside the door of the Sanctuary (as it is represented in the Book), and throw its shadow across the Altar. See where pride leads to even in children of GOD in high estate when they forget the Rock whence they were hewn, the source of their Being; when they forget that they cannot live in the Divine sense except in HIM, from HIM, and through living for HIM. For if we live in HIM and operate from HIM, we must in very deed live for HIM. You cannot *know* GOD and cease living for HIM. It is not possible. To know HIM is to live for HIM. If you do not wish the knowledge of HIM to be veiled within you, and the desire to be altogether HIS changed in you, then put away jealousy and cast out pride.

Tyre, the city of the Prince, once so glorious, lost its riches. The Prince of Tyre, once so holy and noble a Potentate, was carried into bondage. There is a wealth of sacred story we may not even touch the border of at the present time. But I would say this to you as to true Masons of GOD: behold in the ancient times how Solomon and Hiram worked! Not only through the Planetary Hierarchy did they labour, but through all the Sons of GOD who rejoiced in the Prince of Tyre. The FATHER-MOTHER through them administered to you that you might administer and share in the building up of such a Christhood as ye had once known on the Solar Body, and which ye came to manifest upon this once most glorious Holy

City, Ierusalem. For the ancient city of Ierusalem was the reflection of the Eden of GOD, where ye walked, where GOD communed with you, where HE sought through you to lift up all HIS children into like consciousness of HIMSELF, to be the like exposition of HIMSELF, and learn how to share in the like glorious and most noble service.

A GLORIOUS PROPHETIC EASTER DAY

It is Easter morning. It is the most wonderful Easter morning we have had since the Oblation began. Each one becomes more remarkable. The motion (though it is quite likely you but little realize this)—unseen, Elemental and Occult—is tremendous. Why? Because the stone, the rock from the Mountain, has been thrown into the Sea of the Earth, the great Sea of its Astral and Occult atmospheres; and every unveiling of these Mysteries sets the waters of that Sea in motion. The reason for having from time to time to give you a warning note to guard yourselves as you leave such a gathering as this, is not because there is anything awaiting to hurt you, but that the waters have been so set in motion, that you must be prepared for their resurgence upon the shores of your life, even in great rebounds like mighty waves. I would have you glimpse the true meaning of the vision. It is the Resurrection morning, and the Sons of GOD are arising. The Sons of GOD are rising out of the graves of matter to appear in the Holy City of Ierusalem once more. They are coming back to testify of HIS Love and HIS Wisdom. How? By the embodiment of that Love and Wisdom? Oh, such will have to be done, more and yet more by all of you. The real testimony is not in a mere outward proclamation. The real testimony is in the concrete exposition of the life of a Son of GOD in yourself. But in doing this you will not be ostentatious and call attention to yourself as such. No; you must reveal yourselves as Sons of GOD by your actions, in your words, through your gait, in your deportment, and by your attitude to everyone. A Son of GOD cannot be other than like the FATHER-MOTHER.

Everything that savours of other than HIS quality must be eliminated. HIS Love must become triumphant. The real Resurrection of the Being must be accomplished through rising into the glory of the consciousness of HIMSELF.

This Easter Day is a wonderful morning for me and for you; for me very specially in a way no one could understand. There are elements in one's history, and travail in one's Being, and ministries unseen and motions beyond interpretation which none but the Heavens can witness, and none but the Heavens understand. In a degree this is true of each one of you. It is Easter Day for you also. Therefore, I ask you to arise! Arise! Arise! Do you not see the stone is rolled away which prevented the real arising; that Christ is no longer shut up in the grave where the Church buried Him, though you may see the grave clothes there where people still go and dwell mournfully over the past? Christ is risen! Let Him be risen in you! Christ is risen! He has arisen in this world in the measure in which each one of you who knows this great truth, rise to be like Christ who ever is an exposition of the radiance of the FATHER-MOTHER. And in that exposition He is the sum of the Love, the compassion, the pity, the gentleness and tenderness, and the all-embracing ministry of Jesus, the Love-child of GOD. Oh, that I could move you for HIM as I fain would; that I could reveal HIM as my Being yearns to reveal HIM! But in so far as I have been able to do so, will you behold HIM? And in the measure in which I have been able to interpret HIS Will, will you hear HIS Voice and come? Behold! it is the Resurrection hour. Christ, the Solar World in this system, has triumphed. GOD the FATHER-MOTHER, through HIS glorious Body, has triumphed. This world is now on its way to know the joyful sound of the salvation that GOD provides, even the healing of all the wounds of HIS children, and the re-establishing of a realm and a reign within it, of righteousness, equity, and peace, because there is purity and gentleness, tenderness and lowliness, compassion and exquisite overshadowing, defending and endearing pity.

*   *   *   *   *   *

O most transcendent Mystery of Love and Wisdom!
Thou art our Father-Mother.

In Thy regnancy within us Thou art Lord of our Being. The Heavens declare Thy Glory; their motion is full of the Praise of Thee.

The Earth once revealed Thy Glory, ere the great darkness fell upon its Planes. Through its long night Thou hast preserved Thy children unto this Day of Resurrection which Thou hast accomplished through Thy Love in its most Holy Passion.

Thy Children would dwell again in Thee.

Amen and Amen.

THE MESSAGE OF EZEKIEL

A COSMIC DRAMA

*

PART SIX

*

THE PHARAOH OF EGYPT

THE PHARAOH OF EGYPT

You would recognize in the Logia of the Prophet concerning Egypt and the Pharaoh, the close association between the subject matter of it and that of which I spake to you this morning. You would recognize that the description given had relation to *the great descent* and all those who were involved in it. You would sense, in some slight degree, the mystery associated with the terms Egypt, and Assyria, and also with their mighty princes; and if you discerned deeply enough you would recognize how involved the ancients of Elam became in *the great descent*.

Now, in so far as I may be able in this hour, I would unveil to you the inner significance of Egypt with its mighty princes; and the land of Assyria with its great king.

It is not surprising that in the ancient Mysteries Egypt has occupied a large and important place. There were ages when occultism in the form of black magic (an occult power misused) penetrated the whole religious community of the land, and was used by the priesthood and many others. There was a period, however, when the glory of Egypt was known, and even the inner significance of its geographical situation. For the terms which came to be used had spiritual significance. They were full of spiritual meaning. They had their origin in spiritual qualities and quantities, and were applied to the country, to places, and even to individuals, because of the office filled by the individuals and the places, the situation of the villages and cities, hills and valleys, and the land, and even the physiographical formation of the land itself.

It was thus that the present land of Egypt came to be so named, with its marvellous delta and its dual river, the white and the blue Niles. The delta part with a considerable portion south of it was named Lower Egypt;

whilst the sources of the Nile amid the great hills south in Africa, came to be spoken of as Upper Egypt, where Israel once dwelt.

For Israel dwelt in Upper Egypt for ages, teaching the Mysteries. Then they gradually went down into Lower Egypt. Thus Egypt, Upper and Lower, became the home of the Mysteries in the earlier ages; and then Middle and Lower Egypt the home of the Mysteries in the days when the occult powers made use of them for wrong ends.

The Pharaoh of Egypt is the vestige of a great and glorious history and mystery. The word itself is significant, and does not contain within itself the meaning such as we historically associate with the name of Pharaoh of Egypt. There is no oppression in it. There is the mystery of magnetic radiance in it, as we shall see.

THE EFFECTS OF THE BETRAYAL

When this world was betrayed, the Prince of Tyrus was brought down, and the marvellous city of his regnancy became so changed that the heavenly treasures of which it was full were also changed into elemental things in an earthly sense. When the betrayal was effected of the glorious one of whom I have spoken to you, even Lucifer, who lost his vision and went out from the Presence and was brought low, there went down with him, not only his own land, but the kingdom of Zidonia and all its princes; and the descent was even greater than is represented in the prophetic message; for it took them into the nether parts, down into the states of such elemental conditions that they became venues of bondage, veritable hells, scenes of disorder, theatres of conflict, where the drama of life was changed from being a sublime processional of the active forces of the Divine Love and Wisdom producing growth and evolutary acts in the children by which they rose up in their consciousness before the FATHER-MOTHER, to be one of pain and sorrow and spiritual warfare and death. What is known as evolution—spiritual and divine evolution of the Soul—had to be suspended. The result of this tragedy is, that there has been no spiritual growth and evolution on the planes of this Planet for countless ages. All that is thought of in connection with growth and evolution, and associated with the development of the human race through the ages, is but a vista of the endeavour through great aeons on the part of the Heavens to bring the children back, and on the part of the children to rise up out of their fallen states. Though there have been revivals and temporary uprisings of the human race through all the ages, there has always been a submergence again. There have been upheavals, but these have been followed by spiritual submergences, corresponding even to the upheavals and the submergences of the outer planes of the Planet. Even the Ancients of Elam who went down— the Christs of GOD—have never known, since their betrayal into the nether world was fully accomplished, the joy of their ancient estate, except in a very partial way. They have never recovered the transcendent vision that once was theirs. Though they have glimpsed that there was once a great reality in their history, they have never recovered the realization into which they had entered, of the Presence Who walked amidst the Garden of GOD, the real Garden of Eden, since Eden was closed to them after the great betrayal. But they have dreamed of Eden. They have hungered for its life. They have cried out again for the vision that was theirs. The travail of the Christhood has been a travail of ages. They were taken to the Bethlehem from time to time to be renourished, and then sent back for ministry. For they could not, without further disaster to the world, be taken away altogether and placed

where they might rise right up again into their ancient
estate. They have had to remain as the crossbearers
adjacent to this world, and in the heart of it to share, aye,
more than to share, even to carry for the Divine, the
burden of this world's travail. It was because all that
they carried could not effect those changes necessary in the
Astral-Occult Kingdoms, that the Oblation had to be
projected and borne; not because they were deficient, but
because the elemental Titanic forces were too great to be
overcome except by a most special ministry rendered
from the Divine Kingdom, through the Solar World.

In the founding of ancient Egypt many of the ancient
Christhood had a part. Perhaps as I unveil this to you the
meaning of the Delta will open out to your vision. For,
it is said, Egypt represents the body. In the Mysteries it
was the land of the outer manifestation. It was taken as a
symbol of the body. But there was the Lower Egypt,
wherein was the Delta. There was the Upper Egypt,
wherein were the springs of the great river that nourished
the Delta. Egypt was called Egypt because of its con-
stitutional representation of the Mystery of a Human
Soul's formation, and the path, in the form of a delta, of
the Nile of God, the river that is one, then two, then one,
flowing into all the avenues of the life; the finer body or
the Upper Egypt, the denser body or the Lower Egypt.

The arid sands that arose there, came after. The
burning sands were taken symbolically to represent the
effect of the Solar Beam upon the misdirected passional
nature; so the fires of Egypt consumed the Being in an
unredeemed state.

THE PHARAOH RELATED TO THE SUN

Who is the Pharaoh who is said to have been the
oppressor? Those who are always seeking for the fulfilment

of the divinity in them through other than the right avenues or the true and the beautiful ways which are as avenues of the Delta of the Divine fashion within themselves: such are as Pharaoh the Oppressor. Who is that Pharaoh who is great and glorious as a Son of GOD? He is the Solar Beam, as the word itself means in its root—Pharaos, the Sun. For the play of the magnetic forces of the Divine World upon a life that is unredeemed, and yet seeks to bask beneath such Rays, produces in that one such a burning of fires ofttimes spoken of as the Fires of Gehenna. But the action of that Beam is not to create hells. Oh no; it is unto purgation of the life, to the casting out from the life of all those elements which are foreign to the real, living, Divine stream that flowed through the upper land down into the lower, and out through the delta into the great Deep where all things would be, as it were, lost, that is, poured out for ultimate purification, transmutation, and unto the restoration of the elements to their ancient estate.

The oppressive Pharaoh, the prince of an earthly Egypt, is one who makes misuse of the Solar or Divine Energy within himself to oppress, to hurt, to slay, to destroy, those elements and most glorious things which speak of HIM Who is the Living ONE and the Light of Life.

As the Prince of Tyre represented the Divine World and had a Divine name, so Pharaoh represented the World of the Gods, and had a Divine name. He represented the ruling principle within the land of the bodies of the Upper and Lower Egypt.

Behold how perfect the Mysteries of GOD are! Each land has its prince. Each land has its Regal Estate. Each land has its ministry. Each land has a purpose through its ministry to fulfil. Each land has a relationship to the Garden of GOD. Each land belongs to the Soul's constitution. For, as is the macrocosm so is the microcosm, and man is the Divine microcosm. And, therefore, as the Eden of GOD is in the very centre of our magnetic Being, so has the FATHER-MOTHER placed Upper and Lower Egypt towards the realms of the manifestation; yet the Upper Egypt reaches to the great heights whence spring up the streams of the Eternal Mystery to formulate themselves into a river (HIS mysterious River) to flow down through the vehicles, even unto the outermost Delta.

THE MYSTERY OF THE DELTA

What is the mystery of the Delta? It is the arterial life. It is indeed something great to feel the streams of GOD flowing through your body, affecting it as well as the emotion of your Being. It is something most potent to feel the magnetic play of the Solar Beam upon you. And it is something more because much greater, to feel the play of the Solar Beam within you, so that it passes into you and through you, then through all the delta of your vehicles, the white Nile Water of Life mingling with the magnetic blue Water of Life, one source, one river, yet two becoming one and touching every avenue. For the White Nile represents the Stream of the Divine Love as Life, and the Blue Nile as Devotion. No part of your life must be in the least degree divorced from HIM Who is its magnetic centre, its lifestream. All the land of your heritage must partake of HIS exposition. Yes, all of the trees in the Garden of GOD must minister unto the life. They contain food for the Being. They contain exposition of the motion of HIS Sacred Spirit. They contain revelations of the motion of HIS Cross. They are the degrees wherein HE HIMSELF finds exposition in you on the several kingdoms and within your different planes.

How great this mystery is you will see. When the Prince

of Tyrus was betrayed and the princes of Zidonia went down with him, then the land of Zidonia became changed and all the riches of the Heavens took merely earthly significance. The greatly enriched city of Tyrus became a centre of occult merchandise and power and magic. All became changed from things spiritual to elements and powers merely material.

Then was the Assyrian also brought low. It is another mystery term representing the mind that was once most glorious before GOD. For the Assyrian is the mystical representation of the ruling principle of the Understanding in its inward and upward look. The Assyrian who exalted himself to the Heavens was beautiful with the beauty of GOD; but pride of mind brought him down, and the Pharaoh went with him. When the mind falls, all that is beneath it in state falls with it. It is quite obvious when you understand. When the mind falls, all that it should have governed falls with it; for all that is beneath is dependent upon the state of the governor or prince.

Thus it may be seen there is no redemption unless the mind be redeemed. There is no re-elevation unless the mind be repolarized. There is no restitution unless the mind be once more exalted to its Divine Estate. There can be no perfect realization of the Sacred Mystery of the FATHER-MOTHER, unless the mind be one with HIM in the Eden of GOD—one with HIM in purpose; one with HIM in the motion of thought expressed as ambition; one with HIM in the desire to receive HIS glory as HE would shed it, and have the mind shed it and reflect it. For that glory HE would have reflected in a world full of volatile elements, as the radiant exposition of the motion of HIS own Spirit. But that cannot be done in a world whose motions are unto fixity of elements, with the resultant limitations of a bondage begotten of the fixed conditions.

Here you will get another glimpse into the sacred
Mystery of the Fall, not only in the Lower Spiritual
Heavens and occult realms, but even right through to the
outer planes of the Planet. And you may witness how you
yourselves were enmeshed in the great descent, and how
the Ancients of Elam, the Ancients of GOD, were carried
away into bondage. For an Ancient is one who has in
some measure realized the Divine. He is one who is in
the consciousness, in some degree, of a Son of GOD. That
Sonship is expressed first as a Celestial Man, then as a
Son of the Gods when the Soul has attained to high
Celestial estate. When it attains to Celestial estate, it is a
Son of the Gods. By that is to be understood that such
an one has the capacity to function on any member of a
system like this in its unfallen state; and may even have
attained the capacity to function on another system, if
sent thither to minister. That one may have risen to such
heights that he has the capacity to travel in consciousness,
to travel to far-off realms even without leaving the Kingdom of the planet or world where he is ministering.

* * * * * *

The Ancients were the members of the Christhood who
were the Children of the Ancient of Days. This term
expresses another old Mystery. They were members of
the great Masonic Lodge of the Heavens, and had become
Masters. They were not so named; but in their estate
they were masters and past-masters, and even grand-
masters, corresponding in their degree to Angels in various
degrees of realization, and even to Archangels. In their
realms of ministry, corresponding to these high estates
according to the degrees of their consciousness and the
intensity of their realization, they had become as the Gods,
or Ancients. They knew HIM Whom they served.

That is why you yourselves are ever seeking to get back to states of experience of long ago though long lost, and to come up to the vision of HIM. You ofttimes ask: "How shall I come at that vision?" And sometimes you venture the question: "Am I growing and getting nearer?" There are times when you wonder if you have grown at all during these years of your ministry in this life, and especially since you contacted the Message. You ofttimes wonder and ask the Heavens whether you shall ever reach the land you dream of, glimpses of which break upon you in the night watches, and in the quiet times amidst Nature, and in the quiet of your own room.

The reason why you are always crying out in your Being for HIS vision is that ye knew it once. Those were glorious times in the Heavens. They were glorious times even upon the Earth planes, for there was at that time no shadow lying athwart the threshold of any one of you, and no long shadows and deep shadows upon the threshold of the earth; for all the children were full of the joy of life and did indeed dance for very joy.

Ah, many a time in these days of the Return has my vision been honoured by being borne back to that time when the Children of the Kingdom danced before the LORD, rejoicing in their childhood to HIM; when all their service was the exposition of the delight they had in life, and the gladness that was theirs in recognizing and acknowledging their childhood in and before HIM. Your Being ofttimes yearns for that state to come back to you, even in the Egypt of your life, yes, whilst ye are dwellers in the land of the Lower Egypt. For you may be dwellers there and yet be able to reach the Upper Egypt, following the river of the ETERNAL ONE to its mysterious source. For once again are ye to reach the heights in the Upper Egypt, where once you dwelt in the consciousness of H<small>IS</small> Overshadowing, and know H<small>IS</small> directing.

Now you may behold the meaning of this expression with which one of the paragraphs of the text closes:—

O Egypt! O Tyrus! O Zidonia! How great was the fall with which ye were overwhelmed! And how great the travail unto this day!

For when Egypt went down, it fell through the Prince of Egypt going down. He was the representative of the Solar Divinity in the realm of the upper or inner vehicle. And when he fell the lower Egypt also went down. The astral and mental bodies became enslaved. The outer body became captive to all sorts of conditions and elemental forces, the object and victim of inimical powers. Then was it that the children groaned by reason of their bondage. They even groan unto this day, not knowing the reason of it.

THE SUBLIMEST MASS TO OFFER

Then we have that outstanding and glorious prophetic message concerning Egypt and Tyrus associated with the realm of Assyria and Zidonia.

Even out of hell shall the Divine L<small>ORD</small> bring you and all the Children; and ye shall once more be restored with your lands to the ancient estate. It is an enriched Inheritance amid the Garden of G<small>OD</small>. And ye may make manifest again the beauty of the Life and the glory of the Wisdom, the height and the depth of the resplendence of your L<small>ORD</small>.

With this consciousness and vision, beloved ones, before you; with this provoking of you to understand your own history, and the way of the F<small>ATHER</small>-M<small>OTHER</small>; surely there shall be in this day, in this very hour, such an arising of Israel, such an arising of yourselves, as will leave behind all the low things of Egypt, all the impure things associated with fallen Egypt, all the jealousy and the pride associated with fallen Assyria, all things that hurt or destroy; and that ye may ascend again the holy Mount of GOD whereon no such things can abide; and that there ye may realize again the part you have in the world's travail. Yea, more than that; that ye may realize the joyful part you have, in the world's travail unto its Redemption; that ye may be more worthy of the heritage, worthy of having been the Ancients, of having known the Light of Christhood, of having been called the Sons and Daughters of the Gods, the Children of the King, the Princes and Princesses of that divinely royal Regnancy, wherein HE was manifest as King of all the kings, and LORD of them all.

It is an hour throbbing with Divine History. It is an hour vibrant with the Voice of the Heavens calling to you to arise. It is an hour that speaks of Divine possibilities and of the coming Redemption. It is an hour of sublimest consecration. It is the early hour of the Easter Day. We appear before HIS Altar to lay upon it all our Being, to offer our Mass and our Eucharist.

Lord, I am Thine. Everything that is worthy in me is of Thee; it is from Thee. Every potency of value is a power from Thee; it is of Thee. Whatsoever there may be of riches in me are of Thy bestowing. Lord, I am Thine. I would be Thine, from the crown of my Being to the Divine Understanding whereon my feet are planted. I would be Thine, absolutely Thine, in my Being, for Thy Service. I would that there should be nothing lacking in my oblation unto Thee, O my Lord, my Father-Mother.

In the Light of the glory of HIS coming to us, all our travail for HIM is as nothing. All our burden-bearing is HIS own; we are honoured to share in it. Even its sorrow, its pain, the anguish begotten of it, are as nothing in the Light of HIS resplendence and the glorious fulness of HIS coming. Thus would I bear you all with me.

Thus would I marshal you and lead you, bearing you on the Altar of my Being, guiding you in this sublime pilgrimage of Earth ministry for our LORD, making the sacrifice complete, making the ministry perfect, making Zion once more and even Ierusalem, the holiest of GOD's Cities, radiant with HIS Glory shed over all the Earth from out the Cloud of HIS Resplendence.

*   *   *   *   *   *

I trust that though I have had to unveil the tragedy that befell this world, and some of the shadows that still lie athwart its threshold, within and upon you no shadow shall remain. May there be only the resplendence of HIM within the Sanctuary. HE dwelleth there and doth mediate unto you. HIS glory falls upon the threshold, from the Cross on HIS High Altar, even to the outer threshold. For thus the glory within the Sanctuary shall be manifest in the without. Thus there shall be a revealing of HIS own sacred Mystery, from the centre of the Innermost Court to the circumference of the outermost. May these revealings herald for you the Day above all Earthdays, even the Divine Eastertide, not only in the arising of Christ within you, but also through your fuller entrance into the consciousness of your LORD, and the joy HE doth bring with HIM.

Rejoice and be glad! The Prophets live again! MARANATHA!

THE MESSAGE OF EZEKIEL

A COSMIC DRAMA

★

PART SEVEN

★

THE ARISING OF ISRAEL
AND
THE FIRST RESURRECTION

THE ARISING OF ISRAEL

On more than one occasion I have spoken to you on the Vision of the Valley of Dry Bones, though not after its cosmic relationships.

It is a vision portraying the Resurrection, which is a great spiritual Mystery. Resurrection implies a previous state of lifelessness spoken of as death.

The vision is a picture of such a Resurrection as the religious world has not yet come back to dream of. As yet that world is asleep. It is deep in the stupor produced by astral and occult narcotics. Soon it must awaken to the conscious vision of the reality of Divine Things. Here is a vision of cosmic drama, beheld by the Prophet where all cosmic things can be truly beheld and understood. For though many things in the realms of manifestation related to the cosmos may be observed and related, tabulated and studied, yet there is no consciousness of their real inner relationships as well as their outward relationships, unless that consciousness has been illumined in the Realm where alone such illumination could come.

And you will note this, that whilst in many places of the same prophecy it is an Angel who attends the Prophet to show him things and interpret them, in this instance it is said to be the LORD HIMSELF Who appears to him, carrying him up in the Spirit within the spiral of the Divine Whirlwind to the Realm where he could look out upon such a sacred Mystery as is figured forth in the Valley of Dry Bones.

The Spirit of the LORD took him to a Realm where he could understand. He had the power of response within him. He was caught within the Spiral Breath and upborne, and, being so upborne, was carried forward to look out upon many things of the past.

The allegory is brief, but it contains a world of history. It seems as if it were but the picture of some passing episode in the history of a people; whereas the dramatic situations and tragic experiences of all their history upon this world were gathered up into it.

In this vision it is not for one moment to be supposed that the "dry bones" represented an actual state of spiritual death in the people unto whom the prophet would have to speak; but it did represent them in their spiritual experience away from the conscious, vital forces of their LORD. It spake of what they had been. At one time they had been as a mighty army clothed with the Divine Flesh or Substance of Being, and covered with Divine Skin. This latter symbolizes the power of atmospheric pressure by which there is conveyed the power of defence. In this respect they had been a mighty army of Souls in ministry. Many things concerning them had been unveiled to the Seer and the Prophet.

Unto Isaiah there had been shown the state and needs of the people. There had been given to him the promise of the redemption for the whole Planet, and Regeneration for Israel, by means of the Oblation; for he is the Prophet of the Oblation. That was his message given from the Heavens unto the Children of Israel. Ezekiel becomes unto them the Prophet of the Temple of the LORD. He has to show to them again the Divine Temple to be once more built up upon the Earth, and to outline to them its superstructure and the characteristics of the Priesthood to be restored.

In this wonderful vision the Prophet looks out upon the world as it had become. He witnesses the effects upon the Children of Israel. He sees them suffering through bearing unspeakable burdens which made life to them as veritable death. He beheld them far away from the Homeland which was their heritage, sorrowing, filled with the pains of this world's own sins and the burden of its travail, ever crying out for the day when they could come into the Presence of the LORD and ever enquiring when that day would come, though ofttimes growing hopeless because of the outlook and the apparent delay.

Certainly to any prophet looking out upon such a vision there did not appear to be great hope of a mighty army of Souls who would be stalwart in Divine potency and glorious in Celestial embodiment. It looked as if it could not be.

Thus when the Blessed ONE asked the seer,

"Son of Man, thinkest thou that these can live again?" he could not answer. He knew the history. He knew that drama, so many of whose acts and scenes had been shadowed in deep tragedy.

"Lord God of Israel, Thou alone knowest whether it can be so. It seems hopeless, and so I turn to Thee. Thou alone knowest."

And then he was commanded to prophesy that it would be so, that there would actually be the Resurrection of all the House of Israel, that they would all come back again and that the way was being prepared for their return. And in the prophetic vision he was commanded to prophesy unto the Four Winds. *"O Winds of the Lord, blow!"* He was commanded to prophesy that that Breath would blow from the four quarters. And as he prophesied, the Breath came from the four quarters and touched them and they lived. Every one stood upright; and together they formed a mighty army.

THE COSMIC TRAGEDY OF ISRAEL

The drama is cosmic. It portrays succinctly the tragedy that befell the House of Israel within a fallen world. It implies all that the world became when its Edenic life was changed into wilderness and desert conditions, when the Soul was shut out from Edenic fellowship with the Angels, and even the Children of Israel from intimate communion with GOD. So heavy were the conditions, so tragic the motion in the world, that there was no Eden any more for the world's children, nor was there a continuous "walking with GOD" in consciousness for the Children of Israel. So grievous was the hurt that even the Elders of Israel, the eldest among the Christhood who came to this world, could not endure the glory of the LORD when HE appeared in the Cloud of HIS Radiance upon Mount Sinai and upon Mount Horeb. The whole tragedy of the world is gathered up into that vision. For if Israel became as a valley of dry bones, Souls whose whole superstructure, whose uprights, whose ligaments, whose flesh, whose arterial system, and whose covering, had been in the fashion of Celestial embodiments, what must have happened to the children of this world? Fortunately for them they did not reach such heights, and so they had no such deep travail begotten of the passionate memories that broke upon the Soul, from time to time, of a glorious past which seemed forever gone, a past wherein the Soul knew the LORD.

Oh, the travail of this world could not be written. It can be glimpsed from afar off, but known only in the Realm where such things alone can be unveiled. Even the travail of the House of Israel would be hard to tell. No language would be adequate to portray the journeying of the once glorious Christhood down into the deep valleys, or states into which this world had sunk in its life, its vision, and its hope. For they became partakers in the most real sense of the burden of the children of this world, and sharers with them in their suffering. They were the Souls who travailed. A Soul can only travail when the motion of the Divine consciousness in it is great. A Soul capable of travailing tells, in the measure of its power to travail, its own great history; its length of days; the ages inwrought into the fabric of its Being and radiated through its consciousness. It was thus the House of Israel could sorrow as the world's children could not sorrow; could cry out unto the Living GOD as only Souls who had once glimpsed something of that glory could cry out; and yearn for fulfilment as only Souls could yearn who had once realized in great measure the fulfilment of the Encompassing and Overshadowing Presence.

The first view of that picture is a tragedy. Oh, what does it not picture of this world's great descent!

The second view of the vision is one that fills the heart with a great hope. It filled the hearts of the best Sons of Israel, even in those days, though they were not able to take in the far-reaching meaning of all that the Prophet was given to say to them, any more than they did all that Isaiah spake. And we need not wonder at it. For, although we have moved along the time-circles some three thousand years since the time when that vision was supposed to be given, the people do not understand anything more now. Even the Scholars seem at sea. Isaiah is still a sealed book to the Church. So is Ezekiel. They are read, it is true, as Lessons; and they are worked into liturgies; and they are loved for their poetic diction. That is beautiful. But their Message is, even unto this day, as a voice crying in the wilderness to prepare the way for the coming of the LORD.

THE ANCIENT HOUSE OF I-O-SEPH

Now, this cosmic picture we will look at in its individual relationship, and also in its cosmic relationship to Israel. The latter we will take first.

It speaks of the whole Household of Israel. It speaks of that which the ancient Christhood is to become again as a Household.

The ancient Christhood was composed of priests of the Living GOD; every one a priest for GOD. A priest is a mediator. No man can make a priest, however good he is, however high in earthly estate and office. Certainly the schools do not make priests; but they often spoil those who would be exquisitely beautiful in priesthood. That does not mean that all that the true schools should be able to give to those who might minister for GOD, is to be despised. Not so. But the schools must be centres of living forces in order to give vital inspiration to those who would be recipients of such a vision as they hold.

Every one of the ancient Christhood was in priesthood. They were in Holy Orders. Some were in Office; but they were ordained of GOD. That is the real ordination. For, if a man or a woman be not ordained of GOD, he or she is not ordained at all, in the Divine sense. To be ordained of GOD means to be chosen and appointed because the individual has attained to certain spiritual status, and is capable of being the vehicle of the Divine for ministry.

The ancient Christhood was a regal community, because it was of a royal house. It was of the House of Ioseph. I-O-Seph is the Luminous ONE, known as the Luminous Cross. It was HE Who gave to them their ancient titles. They were Princes for GOD. They were GOD's Israel. In their priesthood they embodied the glorious, spiritual Temple of the Heavens. They were, in the ancient days, related to Solomon's Temple. They shared in the cosmic representation of that sublime truth. They were for GOD in this world that which is designated, The Temple of Solomon.

THE REAL TEMPLE OF SOLOMON

The Temple of Solomon is a Temple of the most perfect fashion. It is the Temple of complete and perfect embodiment. It is the Temple of highest priestly ministries. It is the Temple whose precious things are gold; they are fashioned of the Divine Love. It is the Temple of high sacrifice. It is the Temple of the Overshadowing Cloud of His Radiant Presence. It is the Temple wherein is the consciousness of the ever Abiding ONE, Who, through His Overshadowing, illumines all the House of Israel, and makes it radiant from its High Altar even to the outer courts.

On the Earth planes they were that Temple; each one a part of the living whole; each one suffering when any part came to suffer; each one gradually feeling the break as that magnificent, Divine superstructure in manifestation upon the Earth planes, crumbled into dust. That was when there was no longer any cosmic embodiment of Solomon's Temple, no longer a living united Christhood but only scattered members, each member suffering in his separateness and aloneness, each member seeking to get back into a state of unity through the unification of all the parts. It was thus that from time to time they were foregathered. They were brought together that they might help each other as communities. It was thus that they were drawn together amid the ages of travail, feeling a strange, inner relationship to each other as parts of that great Temple, but so hurt that they found it difficult to unify and become one.

SEALING THE HOUSE OF ISRAEL

The Prophet's vision is first cosmic in relation to the whole Household of Israel. He looks through the ages of Travail, and he sees the coming of this Day.

It is the day of the numbering of the House of Israel. It is the day of the Resurrection of the great army of Israel. It is the day when every one of the ancient Christhood shall stand up upon his feet and her feet, a mighty army for GOD. It is the day when the real priesthood ordained

and appointed of GOD shall be restored to serve and
mediate within HIS Temple, even from HIS High Altar,
which is no earthly altar, nor earthly house, nor confined
within the thoughts of an earthly house; but a great,
Spiritual House fashioned within the Divine Atmospheria
by every member rising into living priesthood for HIM,
each one being not only a part of the architectural whole,
which is magnificent, but, in the Office filled, a living
priest for GOD, in whom there is the motion of the Sacred
Flame—that Flame which energizes all the Being from the
innermost to the outermost, even making the outer vehicle
to be a partaker of the Divine Radiance; that Flame which
illumines the Sanctuary so gloriously that the light of it
goes out through the windows of those courts, even to be
made manifest in the life of the Without.

It is a vision, the accomplishment of which, in these days,
was foreseen by Ezekiel and Isaiah. That which Isaiah
had to foretell, had to be accomplished before that which
Ezekiel saw could be realized. The Oblation must first
come, and then the restoration of the whole House of the
Christhood. The Oblation must first be accomplished,
and then Solomon would come back again in all HIS
glory. HE was and HE is no man. The glorious King is
the Living LORD; the Sol of the Divine World, Who, in
every man, becomes the Living Force for Divine embodiment unto manifestation.

This is the day of the Return. The whole House of
Israel are being blown upon by the Breaths. The Breath
is touching every member in this land and in other lands,
though there are many of them in these days in this land.
They feel a new exhilaration. They become conscious of a
new motion, and yet a motion that is strangely familiar.
There is inborne to them that again they are becoming
inspired and illumined; although they may not as yet have

any memory of the past breaking upon their consciousness. The inspired moments seem familiar; and in such they are upborne to Realms where they are at home.

THE FOUR GREAT BREATHS

The Breaths are blowing now; and as every part of them becomes united, the whole House of Israel will realize that it is not only the single Breath that is blowing. The single Breath blows at first; then it blows in dual motion; then in triple motion; and then in fourfold motion.

For what are the Four Winds which are spoken of that are to be loosed? They are the Four Breaths. What are those four dimensions out from the bosom of which the Four Breaths are to be wafted?

There is but one Great Breath, the Eternal Breath. What we call breath on the Earth planes is but the motion of our breathing. But the breath even on these planes is one with the Mystery which it represents on the innermost. Our breathing is a motion. That which we inhale is of vital moment to us. In a perfectly pure atmosphere it has nothing but life-giving power within it; it is of the Divine even on the outer planes. Even oxygen is changed in its effect as it blows as wind from the west or the south or the north or the east. It is changed in its vibratory motion, and, consequently, limited or intensified in its potency according to the realm, the dimension whence it proceeds and the power of its motion for the time being.

If that be true on the outer, how much more so is it on the inner? For the outer is but the exposition in relation to the Planetary motion and its elements of hidden Mysteries. For the Soul must also have its east wind. In the Planet the east wind is rarely welcomed by any one, and this because of the conditions and the motion of the Planet. For the east wind seems contrary, because it blows as if in opposition to the direction of the motion of the Planet. But it is not the fault of the wind; it is the fault of the Planetary conditions. The east wind is really exhilarating. It is divinely inspiring. And if it be so on the outer when it is gentle, how much more so must it be in the Inner Realms?

The Four Winds relate to the motion of the Divine Breath as it proceeds from the Divine World. And if it should come right from the Divine World in great intensity, you are not able to endure its vibrations, and so you guard yourself from it. You close your planes, even as you gather your garments about you when the east wind blows intensely.

The Divine accommodation ·is exquisitely beautiful in everything, and never more beautiful than when in great accommodation. The Breaths have to blow upon Israel. They are blowing. Oh, East Wind of GOD, blow! Oh, North Wind of GOD, blow! Oh, South Wind of GOD, blow! Oh, West Wind of GOD, blow! Then all that comes with these Breaths shall be laden with sweetness and graciousness, rich with the wealth of flowers with the fragrance of Divine Blooms, shedding Divine Perfume.

Those Four Winds will make Israel again a living body. For it is the Breath of the Divine blowing through the outer gates, blowing through the middle courts of the Being, blowing through the inner courts of the Being, and blowing through the innermost court of the Sanctuary. The outer court is the West; the middle court is the North; the inner court is the South; and the innermost of all is the East where the High Altar is. Those who built their sanctuaries with the Sanctuary looking East, and their High Altar Eastward, though facing the West, knew something symbolically; though these things are not thought so much of in these days.

This cosmic vision is therefore specially unto Israel, the whole Household of the ancient People. And every member will know in that perfect day, every other member of Israel, and there will be great re-unions and no more any division; there will be no more any separation; there will be no more broken parts; there will be no more lack of any tribe in Israel; nor will there be any lack of sacrifice. The precious vessels of the Temple of Solomon that had to go down with the fall of the Temple in Babylon, will all be recovered again; they are being recovered now. By the motion of every Soul that arises, they are being recovered. For, with every one who arises all Israel is arising. Therefore this Message is world-wide, for it has to find Israel; specially is it for this land where so many of the ancient Christhood are to be found. And it is for you, Children of Israel, who can respond to it.

THE DRAMA OF EACH SOUL

This is a cosmic vision of all the travail of your own Being in the past ages, and of that which is now to be as the result of the Travail of the Oblation. The LORD HIMSELF hath spoken it.

"Son of Man, thinkest thou that these can live?" " O Lord God, Thou alone knowest." Yes, the Heavens knew that Israel would live some day; but it was difficult to get at them. But the Heavens were not so sure at one time, that this world could be saved.

Oh, if you knew the drama of this world, you would understand the Passion of the Divine Love, and the unspeakable grief of the Heavens. If you understood in the innermost the tragedies that have befallen this world in its journey, you would also know how the Divine Love sorrowed, and wondered whether it would be possible to bring it back again without a dissolution of the whole superstructure of the Planetary constitution. So many speak and write many things that seem hopeful concerning the whole development of life on this world; but they say many things that reveal how little they know. They know not the night that befell this world, and its strange and awful tragedy.

But Blessed be our FATHER-MOTHER, the day of hopelessness is past. "*These Souls of Israel can live.*" In the days of the Prophet it was only anticipated. It was hoped that it would be so when the Oblation was accomplished. The Oblation being now accomplished, the prophecy is beginning to be fulfilled, and so Israel is arising to the Heavens. "There is joy in the presence of the Angels of GOD over one sinner that repenteth," it is said. Yes! But that is not all. Many may repent from their sins without entering into the Sanctuary that is illumined by the Presence. Many may repent from their sins and come to live beautiful and simple and good lives; and such lives would be contributory to the healing of the world; for each individual is a centre of Angelic potencies. But a Soul must needs do that if it has gone into the ways of sin; and there is joy in the Heavens over its return. But have the Angels no joy over other things? Have they no joy when they see the blessed Angelic Superstructures, exquisite in their substance and radiant in their glory, and in their ministry indescribable, taking form upon the Earth in and through every Soul who embodies the LORD? There is assuredly joy in the presence of GOD in the Angelic World over every one of the Household of Israel who returns. Nay more. The Celestial Hierarchies sing praise unto GOD over every one of the real Israel who returns. Because each one who returns numbers another vehicle of the Christhood. Each one who returns is to be a manifestor of Jesus Christ the LORD. Each one who returns is to contribute to the coming of the Advent or the new Manifestation of GOD through HIS Israel when each member shall be in Christhood. Each one who returns comes back into the estate of Jesus Christ to fill a part in the Divine fabric of Solomon's Temple upon this Earth. Therefore each one who returns will make manifest again the glory of the Divine Love that has never failed, that has known no weariness, that has counted a thousand years as but one day, aye, a thousand ages not too long to minister to a world that has gone astray, or even to one Soul upon the world, to bring such back into the consciousness of that Love and the Radiance of that Wisdom.

THE NEW MANIFESTATION

Now, if this return of Israel were an outward thing, if it were to be a church or an institution, or something that was generally recognized, you would find many flocking to be sharers of it. But that is not the way Israel is to be restored. The return of Israel is through the restoration of the life. It is through the restoration of the vision, through the restoration of the Divine motion within the Being, through the restoration of the heart's pulsing in unison with the Divine Love. It is the restoration of that motion which is a living and perpetual Liturgy of Being, because the whole life has become a Sacrament, a holy Eucharist, a blessed Communion, a Divine Fellowship for GOD.

Israel cannot be found in any other way than by the inner motion. Israel cannot be restored in any other way than by the motion of the Winds of GOD, the blowing of the Four Breaths, the realization of the fourfold dimensional Spirit of the Living ONE. Israel could never be restored so completely that bone shall unite with bone, and all the framework be clothed with ligament, sinew, and flesh, and the Divine arterial system have perfect motion and express the living forces of the Divine Presence crowned with a Light that bespeaks the glory of GOD as an Abiding Radiance within the Soul, except through hearing the Voice they once knew, and responding in the motion of their spirit to the call of the Presence. Thus you will understand that, as the cosmic Christhood has to be found and restored, and the high Temple of Solomon rebuilt, it can be accomplished only through the individual. No one can attach himself or herself to Israel, GOD's Israel, whilst their bones are dry upon the planes of spiritual death. For the arising of Israel is the arising of individuals who comprised Israel. The coming back of what is called "bone to bone," part to part, is not only the restoration of the attributes of the individual, but it is the coming back of every Soul who filled a part in that cosmic ministry. So each one must arise! Get your bones vitalized with the marrow of GOD's glorious Mystery. Clothe them anew with flesh—HIS Substance expressed as flesh and sinew, muscle and ligament. Vitalize them with HIS Lifestream blowing from HIS Divine Heart and pulsing forth HIS Life within you. You have the correspondence of HIS Heart in the very centre of your Being, and of HIS Breath with its motion within you. That Divine Stream maketh every part of you to be alive. It doth make all the garments of your Being, your flesh on every plane, living; every attribute a centre of magnetic force having no shadow of the life of the deep valley, but partaking of the Radiance which HE sheds within the Sanctuary where HE dwells, and whence HE looks out and operates in HIS magnetic stream.

If therefore ye would be of Israel, ye must arise. Ye must be alive. Ye must know the Divine Resurrection of Being.

THE FIRST RESURRECTION

For the cosmic picture is also the microcosmic picture. That which Israel is again to become, Israel can again become only in the measure in which the individual members microcosmically become. For the whole is dependent upon the units; even as you yourself, for the completeness and perfectionment of your life, are dependent upon the perfectionment of your attributes and all your powers. For wherein one power lacks, your life as a whole lacks. If one attribute be wounded, the whole life is wounded in that attribute, and suffers. Therefore every attribute of life must be healed to make the life whole. Thus every Israelite must be whole ere the Household of Israel is complete.

Oh, it is a glorious vision! It is a call to a glorious life, a life transcendent, and a ministry the honour of which is beyond all description. And here I appeal to Israel.

Ye are called to high and holy priesthood, to be again GOD's Christhood making manifest for HIM upon this world. For such a manifestation you will see the need for true unity. But you will never get unity through uniformity in anything. Unity is of the Spirit. It is of Love. It is to be found in oneness of vision and purpose. There is no bondage in it. There are no limitations to the flight of the Being in it. It is the Spirit whose all-expansive motion gives to the individual Soul, according to its estate, even the cosmic consciousness of a Planetary and Solar order wherein it can dwell in HIS Presence Who is the Living LORD.

"Son of Man, can these live again?" *"Lord, my Lord, Thou didst know, and so Thou hast made them live again in part; and Thou art bringing them all to live again as a whole."* And behold, a great multitude arose, and they knew such

Divine Unity as they had not known for great ages. And they are to know that unity again in its full splendour. They are to be united once more as children of the Heavens to I-O-Seph. They are to be HIS Christhood.

What Ezekiel saw, Isaiah had foretold should be realized when the Oblation was accomplished. But they saw only in part. What was foretold, the Seer beheld in the Apocalypse. He saw the motion of the Four Breaths when they were loosened. He witnessed the four dimensional Life coming back again in the wonderful inward vision, the exaltation of the mind to its true ministry, the ensphering of the heart from the Divine to be the vehicle of Divine Passion in its earthward motion in ministry unto the blessing of Souls. He saw the great army gathered up as a multitude to be around the Throne. He thus beheld the return of Israel into the consciousness of the sublime regnancy of the Presence within the Household through reigning within each one. He beheld how in the very heart of the cosmic Israel, GOD was everything. Theocracy was restored—the only true form of government. He witnessed them endowed to be HIS oligarchical Priests, Administrators, Interpreters, Manifestors, Revealers, and Healers. He saw them all restored to fill these offices nobly and in deep humility. He saw the great multitude who had come up out of the tribulation and out of the valley of death, once more living and vitalized as Souls resurrected, full of the glory of the Passion of GOD, made manifest around HIS Throne. He witnessed them laying down all their crowns of attainment, all their sceptres of power, all their diadems of potencies and everything they had, in consecration unto HIM. He heard them, as in the ancient times, ascribe to the FATHER-MOTHER all Glory—

Worthy art Thou, O Lord, to receive the honour and the glory, for the Power is Thine; and the dominion and the regnancy of that Power are Thine. Henceforth our life and service shall be the adoration of Thee, the worship of Thee, the praise of Thee, and the blessing of Thy Name, as Thou dost use us in Thy Name unto the blessing of all Thy children.

O wonderful children of the FATHER-MOTHER! Children of HIS still more wondrous Love! Can ye doubt your childhood to HIM which the motion of your Being reveals, and of which your very yearning of Being testifies? Put doubt away as unworthy of one who should trust HIS Love. For HE has once more brought you up out of the valley of spiritual death into the land of HIS own glorious Presence, that you may learn more and still more of the Mystery of that Presence through beholding HIS glory, receiving of HIS power even unto the embodying of all that HE has become unto you and within you.

* * * * * *

Most Sacred One, our Father-Mother; how shall we interpret Thee, and reveal the extent of the motion of Thy Love unto Thy children? May Thine Overshadowing Heavens in this hour, filling this house with Thine own Heavenly Hosts, pour out of Thy fulness upon each child here, so that there may not be one Tribe, nor even one Soul, lacking in Israel to-day.

THE MESSAGE OF EZEKIEL
A COSMIC DRAMA

*

PART EIGHT

*

TEXT & NOTES

*The hand of the Lord was laid upon me, and He upbore
me to the land of Israel in the days when they were God's
Ancients.   There He set me down upon a very high mountain
on the South side.*[1]

*The mountain was as a city encompassed by walls, and
within its inner walls (embrasure) stood the Temple.*[2]

*When the Spirit bore me within the Temple, One, in the
fashion of a man, stood before me.*

*His appearance was radiant as brass burnished and
reflecting the glory of the Sun.*[3]

*In his hand he held a line which was as of flax, and also a
rod as if to measure the Temple.*[4]

[1] To be borne to the Land of Israel in the days when they were the Ancients of God, was to be taken back to the hey-day of their Christhood Manifestation. It was therefore an illumination in the form of *a recovery* by the Prophet. But all *true recovery* is the result of the Hand of the Lord being laid upon the Being. All illumination is from within, and the outcome of the over-shadowing Presence. When the Paraclete is become within the Sanctuary, the Lord can enable the Soul to recover all things.

The very high mountain itself speaks of the Altitude of the Vision. The mountain is, in mystical terms, a state of Divine Consciousness. That implies the power to look into the Divine World and receive from it.

The South-side in all the realms indicates the Soul's Emotion. It also has relation to the direction or venue through which the Divine Passion is manifested.

In relation to Divine Vision, it relates to the expanse of the Soul's vision when called upon to look into the past, and forward into the future. For even in a Planetary sense, in this hemisphere, it is necessary to look due South to take in the arc of the circle of the Sun's motion from East to West, the rising, the zenith, and the setting.

[2] This is a cosmic vision of Adonai. It expresses what might be termed, *a Solar cosmic consciousness*. But though expressed as relating to the Solar Body, it was of the Divine World.

It is a vision of the Holy One within the Temple of Being; for that Temple is built upon the high Mountain of God. It is within the Divine City which is defended by walls or conditions which guard its secrets.

[3] First the vision of the Temple and then of the Presence within it. The fashion of Adonai is that of the Divine Man. He is radiant and glorious as the Sun in full resplendence. In a Solar macrocosmic vision, He appears to fill the Sun; for the Sun is an embodiment of Him upon the sixth sphere, counting from the within of the Divine World.

[4] This is a cryptic indication of the manner in which a Soul is measured. The line of flax is the plummet of Zerubbabel. It is the Divine Balancer of the Spiral of the Being. It is of the Righteousness of God.

He spake unto me, saying:—

'Son of Man, behold with thy vision, hear with open ear, and let thine heart be fully set upon all that is to be unveiled to thee.

Unto this end hast thou been brought hither that thou mightest declare unto the House of Israel those things which are to be shewn unto thee.'[5]

NOTES ON TEXT

The measuring Rod is Aaron's Rod, or the power of High Priesthood. It is the Divine Magic Rod that has power to accomplish all things for the Divine. As the Temple to be measured is that of the Christhood, and this latter estate is one of high priestly ministry in the Temple of GOD, so the Divine Rod of High Priesthood is the gauge by which the Christhood of the three Courts of the Temple are measured, and even the outer Court, named the Court of the Gentiles. For these Courts represent from *the without to the Within*, the objective life or daily round, the state of Jesushood, then Celestial Christhood, then Divine Christhood. The Rod of the Divine Love and Wisdom tests all Souls in their Degrees of Ascension, and measures the extent to which each has realized the Divine Love and Wisdom.

The individual and cosmic Christhood of Israel was once more to be so measured.

[5] Here again we have the emphasis that the Message is primarily for the House of Israel. Only members of the Ancient Christhood could understand such a Message. Though it touched the Life of every individual member of the Household of Israel, yet it was essentially Cosmic. It was Planetary, Solar, concerning the Divine Kingdom and the Cosmic exposition through the Sons of GOD.

In the days when I was a dweller in the land of the Chaldeans, the Word of the Lord came unto me.[1]

Then were the Heavens opened, and in Vision was God revealed unto me.[2]

As I looked into the Heavens, I beheld a Spiral Cloud whose motion was like a whirlwind with an enfolding Flame.[3]

NOTES ON TEXT

[1] The land of the Chaldeans, though having an apparent reference to ancient Babylonia, was not a province of the Earth. It had relation to the Mysteries. It was the dwelling-place of those who were Magian. It has been said in occult philosophy that all the Mysteries found in the Scriptures of the Old and New Testaments were collected in and transmitted from the land of the Chaldeans.

In this statement we may see a vestige of the Great Truth as occultists have interpreted it. The supposed founder of the Jewish race and religion is said to have belonged to Chaldea. For it is recorded that Abraham belonged to Ur of the Chaldeas.

In this very statement a profound Mystery is hinted at. For Ur of Chaldea signifies the Sacred Fire; and a true Chaldean is a dweller in Ur—the land of the Sacred Fire. That relates to one of the Mysteries of the Innermost Realm of which URI-EL is the Archangel.

It is thus that Abraham of Ur is a Divine Name and represents a Divine Estate.

The Prophet is said to have been in the land of the Chaldeans when the transcendent vision was unveiled to him. This is illuminating.

[2] When the Word of the LORD comes to a Soul, HE comes by means of the Heavens Within. All illumination is from within. Even a Vision such as this having an apparent objective aspect, is entirely subjective. The degree of transcendency is in harmony with the measure of the capacity and estate of the illuminated one. The degree of the Vision is the resultant of the Soul's realization.

No Heavens external to us have the veils drawn which conceal their Mysteries so that these may be looked upon and understood, in any other way than by means of the Heavens within us. *God is seen in high realization.*

[3] This relates to the Divine World. It is a portrayal of the formation and motion of that World. The Divine Secret is contained in the Arche or Principle of the Universe of Being; and this is made manifest in the Spiral. Behind the manifest fashion of all Staral and Planetary embodiments lies the secret of GOD in the Spiral. The Mystery is carried through into the Human Soul whose fashion and attributes are the outcome of spiral motion.

The enfolding Flame is of the Sacred Fire, and is the Auric Cloud of Radiance resulting from magnetic motion.

It was enveloped in Radiance which proceeded from out the midst of the Flame, and was like pure Amber in its colour.

From out of the Spiral there emanated the Four Living Ones.

These had the countenance of Adonai when He appears as the Divine Man.[4]

Each of these had four Faces and six Wings.

Their feet were as standards of burnished brass, and reflected the Glory of the Radiance of the Flame.

Their Hands were like those of a Man, and they placed them under their Wings.

Their Wings were united to each other; for their powers were in unity, and moved together wheresoever they went.[5]

⁴ The Four Living Ones, sometimes spoken of as Living Creatures, have intimate relationship to the Eternal Mystery. They represent the Four Eternities whose central principle is the Arche. They are also expressed in the Macrocosmic Cross whose Four Arms speak of the Fourfold Directions—East and West, North and South. They are the same as the Four Living Ones of the Apocalypse who served before the Throne and adored God.

They had their motion from the Divine Spiral and were in the image of Adonai.

When Adonai appears as the Divine Man He assumes the anthropomorphic fashion, because the correspondence of Him in that fashion is within the Principle or Arche of the Soul.

The Four Eternities are thus gathered up into the Adonai, for all Divine Motion proceeds from Him, and all the Dimensions have their Apexes in Him and circumferences from Him.

Even in a Celestial sense as well as in a Divine sense, El Adonai is the centre of Universal Being; and, expressed microcosmically, He is the centre of the universe of the Soul.

⁵ Wings are symbolic of Powers. They are cryptic. Three sets of Wings denote power of motion as in flight; power to cover as in veiling the Divine Mystery; power to realize the transcendent Mystery as expressed in Divine Awe.

Every Divine Embodiment is thus endowed. Every embodiment of the Divine Mystery is for Service. Wheresoever the Spirit directs the endowed one proceeds. Every embodiment is full of the Divine Awe. There is no irreverence in the Heavens. The Gods have the gift of laughter, but they are ever full of reverence. The Awe of the Lord who is the God of Sabaoth, imbues each one. They therefore at times appear to cover their feet and their hands with their Wings. From all irreverent gaze, the most sacred Mystery as embodied in the Gods, is veiled. For the Hands speak of the Divine Centrifugal or creative motion, and the Centripetal or fashioning process. And the Feet speak of the Divine Understanding in its dual aspects, which like burnished brass can act in an interior direction or an exterior ministry, like a speculum, and reflect the Divine Glory.

The meeting of the Wings signifies an overshadowing and also expresses the Divine Oneness of all motion in the fulfilment of the Divine Purpose.

The likeness of the four Faces of each of the Living Ones was that of a Man as they stood upright; on the right side the face of a Lion; on the left side the face of an Ox; and beneath they had the appearance of an Eagle.[6]

Two of their Wings stretched upwards, and two covered their body.

In their motion they went forward; whithersoever the Spirit directed they proceeded.[7]

And in their motion there seemed to be the appearance of four Lamps whose Flame was as a living Fire moving up and down within the Spiral of the Living Ones; and from out the Flame there emanated great radiations as when it lightneth.[8]

[6] The Four Faces of each of the Four Living Ones make up a strange combination. In mythology each has been deified. Man has been translated to the realms of the Gods until the ETERNAL HIMSELF became as a Man. But also the Lion, the Ox, and the Eagle have found a like place.

Occultly they represent the Physical, the Astral, the higher Mental, and the Spiritual—the order being, the Ox, the Lion, the Eagle and the Man.

In the story of Israel as told in the Old Testament the like imagery is used to describe the four great divisions of Israel. Upon the four Chief Banners the insignia were—on the West side of the square formation, Ephraim the Ox (West side); Judah, the Lion (East side); Dan, the Eagle (North side); and Reuben, the Man (South side).

Celestially they are of the nature of Taurus, Leo, Libra and Aquarius.

Divinely they speak of the Divine Purpose, Power, Righteousness and Equity, and the Baptism of Aries, the Lamb of GOD.

In the Eternal World they represent the Divine Elements of the alchymists—Earth, Fire, Air and Water. But these Elements are constituents of the Divine Ætheria out from the heart of which all Things (Souls, Planets, Suns and Systems) have become.

· It is thus that the Four Living Ones have Eternal Motion and encompass the Four Divine Dimensions.

The Firmament was upheld by the Four Eternities, and it looked like Crystal full of Mysterious Fire—URIEL.

[7] This is true of the whole cosmos. It is the Spirit or Breath flowing out from the Divine Spiral that gives motion and direction. All the Elements in the Divine World are alive. They are full of the vitality of the Eternal. They respond immediately to the Divine Thought or Will. They are in their first or primal state. From them the Divine Ætheria becomes manifest.

[8] In their motion the Four Living Ones had the appearance of four Containers of the Sacred Flame that moved up and down the Spiral; for the Four Eternities or Divine Dimensions are the Lamps or Containers of the Eternal Mystery out from whose Bosom the power in the manifest Universe proceeds. The great radiations proceeding from the Sacred Flame are the magnetic streams generated by means of the motion of the Divine Spiral. Such radiations, according to the degree of the Planetary constitution,

The
original
Fashion
of the
Planet

And the motion of the Living Ones was such that they went forward and returned with the rapidity of a flash of lightning.[9]

Now, as I looked upon the Four Living Ones, behold there appeared a Wheel that was fourfold.[1]

The Wheels were the colour of Beryl, and were contained within each other, like wheels in the middle of wheels.

When they moved they proceeded upon their four sides, and they turned not in their motion.[2]

Their centres were as exalted rings, and their spokes were full of eyes.[3]

When the Living Ones proceeded, the Wheels went with them; when the Living Ones moved above the Earth, the Wheels were likewise lifted up.[4]

would also proceed from the Poles of this world if they were perfect in their polarity. The Aurora Borealis are the vestiges of such potencies. The Aurora Streamers are magnetic; they proceed from the magnetic Pole, and are reflected in the Planet's Vortexya.

⁹ From the preceding statement concerning the nature of the Aurora Borealis, this will be more easily apprehended. The rapidity of transmitted power within the Divine Kingdom is greater than that of Light-Rays within the Celestial. The motion of the Four Living Ones is that of the Eternities.

¹ The four-fold Wheels or Rings represent the four visible Planes of the Divine World. Their formation is like Rings attached to and dependant from the Divine Spiral. The vision is Macrocosmic. It is also related to the Solar Body. These Wheels are visible only to one who is a high Initiate. For the Secrets of the Divine World must needs be guarded. And this has been specially so since the betrayal of this World. For then the Tree of Life in the midst of the Garden had to be guarded.

² The Wheels were the colour of the precious stone Beryl. Now, Beryl is pale-green, light-blue, yellow and white. They therefore represented the Mystery of the Sea (aqua marine), the Mystery of the Firmament (pale sapphire), the Mystery of Gold as that is related to the Divine World (the topaz), and the Mystery of the Primal Light whence all colours of Rays proceed (the diamond). And they moved upon all their sides, because within and without, above and beneath, they were volatile and vibrant, and were so magnetically constituted that they in every way responded to the Law of the Spirit.

³ The central exalted Rings is a cryptic statement of the spiral Mystery at the heart of each Plane. The spokes connecting the Felloes with the Spiral having eyes looking in every direction relates to the Divine Omnisciency penetrating all the planes, and giving to all the true Science.

⁴ Here we have a picture of the Solar action upon the Earth. The Divine World action through the Solar Body affects the Planes of Judah—the Planet-Soul. A world like this is fashioned by means of the action produced through the magnetic motion of the

And whithersoever the Spirit gave direction, they had their motion, for the Spirit in them responded; and the Wheels went with the living Ones; for the same Mystery that was in the Four Living Ones, was in the Wheels.[5]

I also beheld that the Firmament stood above and rested upon the Heads of the Living Ones; the Firmament was like a great Crystal on Fire.[6]

The Wings of the Living Ones were stretched out under the Firmament.[7]

And when they proceeded the noise of the motion of their Wings was as the meeting of Great Waters, and as the Voice of the Omnipotent One when He speaketh to the Hosts of the Heavens.[8]

Four Eternities—the Living Ones. When the Planes of a Planetary World have motion for generative purposes, they are not only held in the Planet's Spiral, but they are effected from and directed by the Divine World through the Solar Body. The Planet's Planes at one time had power to move up and down the Spiral. When the Living Ones overshadowed the Planet, the Planes were magnetically updrawn.

This Planetary glimpse is of most valuable and profound import.

[5] Here we get back to the Eternal World to witness the Divine Unity of the Four Living Ones with the Wheels and the Spirit. For the same Divine Mystery of the Four Living Ones is also in every Plane. The Presence is Immanent in all.

[6] The Four Living Ones being the Four Eternities and Dimensions form the Macrocosmic Cross. The Firmament is represented by the Circle embracing the four Arms, or resting upon the Apeces of each Arm. These Arms are the Heads of the Living Ones.

The Firmament becomes a Sea of Crystal, for the magnetic action from the Divine Centre fills it. *It is the Luminous Cross.*

[7] Here is a Cosmic Picture of the nature of the Living Ones. By their outstretched Wings they formed the Grand Masonic Arch—the overshadowing Arche. This is the Eternal Arch that has no Keystone because all the stones are equal. It is the Masonic Royal Arch of the Divine Kingdom beneath and within which the high Initiate attains Nirvana, in which state the Soul dwells evermore in the Consciousness of the Divine Overshadowing and Indwelling.

[8] The motion of the Elements within the Divine World is the resultant of magnetic action. This is said to be as the meeting of many waters, and as the Voice of the Eternal; because all magnetic action upon the Divine Spheres is unto the fulfilment of the Eternal Purpose; and the effect of the magnetic action upon the gloriously rarefied atmospheres is to give intonation—the Voice and Message of the ETERNAL LORD.

There is also just a glimpse here of how the Divine World

When the Living Ones stood still, they let down their Wings.

And from out the Firmament the Voice spake to them as they stood with Folded Wings.[9]

The
Mystery
of Adonai

Above the Firmament that was over their Heads, I beheld a Throne come into my Vision.

It was in appearance like a great Sapphire.[1]

And upon the Throne and yet above it, I beheld the One Who was in the likeness of the Divine Man.[2]

He was enveloped in a Flame of Sacred Fire whose colour was like pure Amber.

The Sacred Fire moved from His Loins upward, and from His Loins downward; and as it moved it clothed Him with Resplendence.

And the Radiance was as the Rainbow round about the Throne; and it became a Cloud of Glory. For the Rainbow was the Glory of the Elohim.[3]

communicates with the Celestial Hosts. Concerning this latter, more will be unveiled bye and bye.

[9] In this statement there is a cryptic hieroglyphic presentation of centripetal action in the Divine World, and the guarding of the Divine Mystery. It is a great moment even for an Initiate, when he is so addressed from the Divine World. Within him the Divine Secret is guarded.

[1] The Throne above the Firmament speaks of the regnancy of the ETERNAL ONE over all things. HE fills the whole Universe of Being. HE is the Sum of all embodiments in all the Worlds, and reigns in and overshadows all. Though universal in nature and in the Mystery of HIS regnancy, yet HE becomes to the high Initiate who enters into the realization of HIM, particular and even individual. For the transcendency of the ETERNAL ONE in HIS Universality of Immanent Being becomes also in an individuated sense HIS Immanence within the Initiate.

The appearance of the Throne as Sapphire is a revelation of the real nature of magnetic Light—even within the Divine Kingdom.

[2] This is another vision of EL ADONAI—the LORD, the GOD of Sabaoth. Even the exalted Throne is beneath HIM. At first it might seem as if the Prophet were stressing the description, for if a writer were portraying a King and his throne it would seem quite sufficient description to say that the King sat upon his throne, which would also imply that the throne was beneath him. But such a portrayal of the Eternal Mystery would be altogether inadequate. HIS Throne is above as well as within the Innermost Firmament, and in HIS Regal administration HE is always above and beyond the Seat of HIS Regnancy. Even the Firmament where HIS Throne is said to be, is contained within HIMSELF.

[3] This is a marvellous portrayal of the Mystery of GOD. HE is as Sacred Fire in HIS transmutory and energizing motion. HE is thus depicted as the ratifying Fire that consumes the sacrifice upon the Altar.

The Flame was the colour of pure Amber; its auric glory was of the sacred Mystery of Gold. Gold is not a metal, though it is so designated for purposes of differentiation and classification

When I beheld this, I bowed my Being before Him; and then did I hear the Voice of the Presence speaking to me.

And He said unto me, 'Son of Man, stand upon thy feet, and I will speak with thee.'[4]

And I felt the motion of His Spirit within me as He raised me up to stand upon my feet, so that I was able to hearken unto what He spake unto me.

And He said, 'Son of Man, behold! I set thee as a Watchman over the House of Israel.[5]

Therefore hear ye My Word, and proclaim it unto the House of Israel.'

Then I beheld a Roll written within and without. The Writings bore the signs of grief, sorrow and anguish; and these were concerned with the House of Israel.[6]

through the Mystery of its real nature being hidden. It belongs to a class of Divine Elements whose chief use is within the Angelic Kingdoms of all Worlds. It is contained in the elements which comprise the Sun's Photosphere and Chromosphere.

The downward and upward motion of the Divine Flame express the dual action in the Divine Kingdom, which we designate as centrifugal and centripetal. The dual Solar Mystery is here cryptically stated. The downward is the outgoing or creative action; the upward is the ingathering again of the projected energies.

Auric resplendence is begotten in all Worlds and even in the human Soul, through this same dual motion of the magnetic stream.

[4] To hear the Divine Voice and receive a Divine Message it is necessary to stand upright, to be in a state of Righteousness and Equity. For only in such an attitude and state has the Soul power to ascend into the Celestial and Divine realms.

[5] "A Watchman over the House of Israel." This was no light honour, for it carried with it grave responsibilities. He was to be a recorder and director. The mystical watchmen were Prophets and Seers. Who was this Prophet to whom was given the name Ezekiel, and who was qualified to be appointed Watchman over Israel? He was the son of the High Priest of Israel, and himself a Priest. But the real High Priest of Israel was ADONAI, and Ezekiel was a Son of ADONAI in his estate. He was a Messenger unto the House of Israel. But his message had relationship also to the House of Ya-akob-El.

[6] The Roll was the script of the Word of the LORD. It was written without and within. The writing without was the call to Israel; the writing within contained the Mysteries set forth in the Message. The writings bore the signs of grief, sorrow and anguish, because they were related to the great Planetary Betrayal; the fall of the realm of Lucifer; the disaster which befell all the planes of the Planet and her children upon them; the loss of the Christhood manifestation through the Sons of GOD owing to the Planetary changes; with other correlative celestial changes and even Solar and Lunar tragedies.

And the Voice commanded me to eat the Roll. Unto me as I ate it, it was even as Honey; but soon it became bitterness unto me.[7]

A Vista
of the
Divine
Passion

And He also said unto me, 'Son of Man, receive now into thy Heart all of My Word that I shall speak to thee, and hold the things in thy remembrance.'

And His Spirit held me up within the Heavens; and I heard again the Voice of many saying—'Blessed be the Glory of the Lord which proceedeth from Him.'[8]

I likewise heard again the motion of the Wings of the Living Ones, and the vibrations of the Wheels as they moved in unison with the Living Ones.

And as the Spirit upbare me, the bitterness of the grief, sorrow and anguish written within the Scroll, filled me till I became one with them.

For the Hand of the Lord was great upon me even to the moving of the Passion of my Being.[9]

The Grief of the Heavens was profound; the anguish of the Christhood, immeasurable; the darkness in the Planet, terrible.

⁷ To eat the Roll of the written Word was to appropriate the meaning by making it part of the Being. The initiate must ever live by the Word of GOD; and when he is exalted to the Prophetic Office, the Message given him to convey and unveil must first become one with his own substance.

What the Prophet received to unveil to Israel might well fill him at first with the sweetness of Divine Joy; for the transcendent vision was glorious. But as the hidden writings became known through realization, the consciousness of all that had befallen this world and the House of Israel, brought to him the bitterness of unspeakable sorrow. It would be difficult to imagine any Prophet like Ezekiel coming to the consciousness of such things without sensing deeply the bitterness of the betrayal.

⁸ No one could stand upon the threshold of the Divine World because of the intensity of the vibrations, unless upheld by the Spirit.

The proceeding Glory of the LORD is HIS Auric outflow.

⁹ The Prophet not only sensed the Divine Grief, but also became a sharer of it. The Passion of the LORD moved within him till he came to identify himself with its motion and purpose.

Then, in the Firmament that was above the heads of the Cherubim, I beheld the Sapphire Stone that was in fashion like a Throne.

And I heard the Lord God speak unto one who was clothed in fine linen, and say unto him:—[1]

'Move in between the Living Wheels which are under the Cherubim, and fill the hollow of thine hand with the glowing Fire which is between the Cherubim, and scatter the glowing embers of Fire over the City.'[2]

And I saw the one clothed in fine linen go in between the Living Wheels which were beneath the Cherubim.

These stood on the right side of the House when he went in; and the Glory of the Lord filled the Inner Court through the overshadowing Cloud.[3]

NOTES ON TEXT

[1] This is a Solar Vision. It is a description of the action within the Divine Kingdom of the Sun as ministry is rendered to the Earth.

The Throne of the Eternal is Sapphiric. The Seat of HIS regnancy is as a glowing Stone of Divine Azure. An eminent scientist has even affirmed in these days that the colour of the Sun is Blue and not Golden, and that the latter colour was the result of our atmosphere. This is interesting though scarcely correct as a scientific statement. The Sun belongs to the order of the second Elohe, counting from without, or the sixth counting from within. Its Tincture is therefore the Golden Ancient Sardius Stone, though it has also within itself all the Sacred Tinctures: its Aura is Golden. But in its interior realms the Sapphire represents the Divine Regnancy. It is the Tincture of the Inner Firmament.

The Presence clothed in fine linen represents a Solar embodiment of ADONAI. He had attributes to enable him to touch the Eternal Mystery and make transmutory use of the Divine Elements.

[2] The Divine Purpose concerning the Earth is here unveiled. The Servant of the LORD could move amongst the Cherubim and endure the motion of the Living Wheels. These latter were the inner Planes of the Solar Body. The Mystery itself was between the Cherubim in the form of Glowing Fire. The Servant was commanded to take of that Fire and cast it over the City. On the surface it looks like a vestige of the Sodomic tradition wherein it was said that the LORD rained Fire from Heaven upon the Cities of the plains. But the Sacred Mystery is here veiled. The Fire is the Eternal Energy, and the City is the Ierusalem that was once the Holy City of this world's Spiritual Household.

[3] He moved in amongst the creative and distributive Planes of the Solar Realm. The Cherubim overshadowed these. In the motion of these Planes, or Living Wheels, the Divine Purpose is expressed and fulfilled.

The Living Wheels standing on the right side of the Sanctuary imply centrifugal action; for the right hand and arm represent creative potency. But even on the Solar Body all motion unto

THE MESSAGE OF EZEKIEL

Then the Cloud of the Glory of the Lord rose up above the Cherubim, and overshadowed the threshold of the House;

And the whole House became filled with the Radiance of the Lord, from the threshold to the Innermost Court.[4]

The sound of the motion of the Wings of the Cherubim was heard even to the outer court; it was as when the Omnipotent God doth speak.[5]

Then I saw one Cherub put forth his hand from the midst of the Cherubim, and take of the Fire and put it into the hand of him who was garmented with linen.

And he who had received the glowing Fire, went out from the midst of the Wheels which were beneath the Cherubim, and scattered the Fire upon the Earth.[6]

178

the accomplishment of the Divine Purpose is overshadowed by the Cloud of Radiance called the Glory of the Lord. Though a Divine World itself, yet no ministry would be thought of apart from the Divine Presence and His overshadowing.

[4] The Cherubim belong to the Innermost Realm. They are of the Most Sacred Mystery in the Tabernacle or Ark. But the Cloud of the Radiance has within its office the complete overshadowing of the Sanctuary as well as the Shekinah. The Glory of the Radiant One shed within is also extended to the outer threshold. In the perfect constitution of World or Human Soul, the Glory at the Centre radiates to the circumference.

[5] If when the Atmospheres of the Earth have received into them elements which have to be changed, and the process of changing those elements by means of the action of the Sun upon the magnetic vortexya of the Earth results in Lightning and Thunder, what must be the effect within the Sun of the Divine Motion of all its Planes as these move up and down the Divine Spiral, and outward and inward as the nature of the ministry requires. The effects must be tremendous. The Mystery of the intensification of the solar activity for magnetic output, is wrapped up in the motion of the Wings of the Cherubim as these direct the Living Wheels. In their motion doth the Omnipotent speak.

[6] Here is indeed a Rain of Fire. This is a special ministry. The ordinary and regular ministry of the Divine World through the Solar Body, is by means of the Photosphere; but all the special ministries are rendered through what are known as Sun-spots. And twice every year, a most special ministry is given to the Earth as she passes through the Divine World magnetic stream during the Equinoxes.

It is recognized in advanced scientific circles that during the periods of large Sun-spots and at the equinoxes, the whole Planet is greatly affected. But science does not recognize anything spiritual in this. No Divine Action is observed; no Divine Purpose in process of fulfilment is glimpsed. Everything in the vision of physical science is material. The place of God in these ministries is not understood. Indeed, those in the Scientific World who give Him His true place in the motion of the potencies

*Then I again beheld the four Wheels which accompanied
the Cherubim.*

They were the colour of Beryl.

*Though each Cherub had a Wheel attached to him, yet they
all seemed as if they were Wheels within Wheels.*

*And their motion was fourfold; in their motion they
required not to turn round, for they could move in the four
directions.*[7]

*And I heard the Wheels addressed by the Voice of Him who
sat upon the Sapphire Throne; for He commanded them in
their motion.*

*And at His command the Wheels unveiled themselves unto
me: one had the face of an Angel, another was featured
like a Man; one other had the form of Leo in the Celestial
Heavens, and the fourth was veiled to sight, for it contained
the Mystery of the motion of the Wheels.*[8]

*Then I saw the Wheels lift up the Cherubim above the
Earth: their motion was one, for whithersoever the Wheels
went the Cherubim accompanied them. In equipoise and in
their fourfold motion, they were as one. For the same
Spirit of Life was in them.*

*Then I witnessed the resplendence of the Lord which filled
the threshold withdrawn and passed to the place of the Cherubim; and these rose into the Heavens through the motion of
their wings, until they reached the Eastern door of the Divine
Sanctuary and stood equipoised beneath the Canopy of the
Glory of the God of Israel.*

*It was like the Vision that came to me when I was by
the river Chebar. The forms and motion of the Wheels and
Cherubim were the same; and the Glory of the Lord, the God
of Israel, was revealed by them as they obeyed His Will and
moved according to the motion of the Spirit of Life.*[9]

of the Universe, are few. Yet even the fiery streamers that are projected from the Photosphere are the resultants of the Living Wheels or Divine Solar Planes, and the Overshadowing Cherubim of the LORD of Glory.

[7] Here the above truth is emphasized. The Cherubim are represented as riding upon one of the Living Wheels. Yet all the Wheels appeared to be so intimately related to each other that they were as various Rings within one another. Equatorially, all the Wheels or Planes could appear within each other when apparently at rest. From that Solar Centre each Plane in its ministry would move up and down the Spiral. They also contained within themselves the Mystery of the Four Dimensions.

[8] Just a glimpse here of how all perfect motion is the result of the Divine Command or Law. Within the Celestial Realms that Law operates in what has been named *gravity;* also in Spiral motion within each Sun and its system. And it is the same Law that is obeyed in the magnetic motion of the Planes.

[9] Here we have a remarkable cryptograph of the special ministry of the Divine World through the Solar Body to the Earth, and the return of the Divine Hierarchy to the Divine Kingdom of the Sun upon the completion of the ministry. It is truly a revelation of the Resplendence of the GOD of Israel!

Then the Angel brought me again unto the door of the Eastern Court and shewed me Waters issuing from under the threshold.

These Waters flowed Eastward.

They came from under the right side of the Sanctuary, and flowed from beneath the South side of the Altar.[1]

Then the Angel brought me to the Gate that looked Northward and led me thence to the outermost Gate which looked Eastward, and behold there ran the Waters which had issued from the right side of the Sanctuary and flowed beneath the South side of the Altar.[2]

Then the Angel, carrying the measuring Rod in his hand, went forth Eastward, taking me with him.[3]

[1] This is a most fascinating Vision. It is arresting and profoundly moving. That it is a cryptograph the Mystic will recognize. It relates to the Divine Mystery of the Eternal Being and has a particular and a general application. The vision is cosmic; but its apparently personal and individual application as portrayed in the Vision, veils its Cosmic Mystery.

It is the River of the Divine Magnetic Stream—the warm Divine Gulf Stream of the Celestial Heavens in which the Solar Body may be said to float, though it is really upborne by it. It is, therefore, ensphered with its Waters. And the Sun also becomes the vehicle of the distribution of the magnetic stream. It flows through the Divine Ecliptic.

It is that same Stream in which the Planet once moved before the great Descent or Fall. And it is the river of magnetic Solar output which it enters at the approach of the Equinoxes, and passes through, covering a period of about eight days in its journey.

[2] It is difficult to dissociate the term East, from our geographical concepts. Yet it has to be done. Though we use the four terms, East and West, North and South, to describe situations and positions, yet we know that there is no permanent East or West. For the far East from where we may be, becomes West when the pilgrimage is made still farther East. Thus, the use of the term is only a local directional.

All light proceeds from the East unto the West, and from the West to the East; but the magnetic Poles producing the light are North and South. This is a Divine Mystery which will be more fully unveiled in another volume.

From the Eastern position, the right side of the Sanctuary is the North. This description is correct in detail, for the river flows from the Magnetic Pole of the Being as well as in the Inner Worlds; and Southwards from the Altar of Oblation; for the South represents the Divine Passion's outflow.

[3] The Rod is the same as that with which the Temple of the Christhood is measured. It is the Rod within the Ark of Testimony. *It is the Divine Power brought forth from its secret place of the Ark of Being.*

The motion is first Eastward, for that is the primary direction.

With his Rod he measured 1,000 cubits. And he took me through the Waters; in depth the Waters were up to my ankles.[4]

Then he measured with his Rod 1,000 cubits and took me into the River; the Waters were up to my knees.[5]

After this the Angel stretched forth his Rod and measured another 1,000 cubits. And he took me into the River and through the Waters; here the Waters rose to my loins.[6]

[4-7] These paragraphs signify great Mysteries. They speak of the capacity within man of his dimensional consciousness; of the four great Kingdoms within the system; of the four Divine realms within which man has the capacity to reign; and of the four-square city.

The waters in their flow and depth are accommodated to the capacity of man, to the degree and intensity of his consciousness; to each of his four Kingdoms; and to each of the four realms of his regnancy.

They are likewise accommodations to the Planet. The cubit is a Mystical measurement; and the four times separate 1,000 cubits, express the attainment of Nirvana when the Soul can move within the Great Deep.

The Waters to the Ankles signify that the Soul's Understanding bathes in the Divine Stream, or that it must do so on its journey. For the Feet signify the Understanding of the Mind with its dual Arch as expressed in the instep. And the Arch in combination with the Ankle, are reminiscent of Spiritual Motion. Though on the outer planes we may make carriages to convey us from place to place, in the Spiritual realms we must know the power of the Understanding to take flight in thought and service.

[5] The Waters to the Knees show a much higher degree of realization. They are intimately related to the Ankles and Feet, but are greater in their range of service. And they carry the Soul into the realm of high devotion such as obtains within the Angelic Kingdom. The Angelic World is a realm of Prayer and Spiritual Mediation. By its activities are the Etherial Sanctuaries raised. In our Being we *bow* in Prayer. The attitude expresses humility and reverence. And everyone must know the River at its Station where the Waters are knee deep; for there is no true growth without humility and reverence.

[6] Another great degree caused the Waters of the River to rise to the Loins. This is the Celestial Estate. The Creative forces and powers have not only to be purified as in the first and second Degree, but they have to be consecrated absolutely unto the service of the Divine. When a Soul would enter the realm of the Gods, all its powers must needs be laid on the Altar of Oblation. In the Loins lies the magnetic Pole that connects us with the Solar world: the Initiate must be in unity with that world.

The Mystery of all these Degrees is also great; and they relate to the Planetary Manifestation—of which more elsewhere.

Once more the Angel took me with him as he measured by his Rod yet another 1,000 cubits; but here I found the River so deep that I could not walk through its Waters. The River had become so deep and so great that only those who were great swimmers could enter its Waters. Nor could it be encompassed.[7]

The Two
Pools of
Wisdom

And the Angel said unto me, 'Son of Man, understandest thou this Mystery of God?'

And I was so filled with great Awe at the wonder of the mysterious River, and because of my experiences in its Waters, that the motion of my Being could not find any utterance.[8]

Then I beheld on the banks of the River many Trees. These clothed both sides.

And the Angel said to me, 'Wheresoever these Waters flow, healing is brought to the Earth's streams, and to all Souls.

And the Fruits of the Trees shall be for meat unto all Souls; the Leaves also are of the Everlasting.

And the Fishers of Souls shall sit upon the Banks of the River, from En-gedi even unto En-eglaim.

And the Great Fish shall be found there.'[9]

The 1,000 cubits make the cube of 10. Ten is a mystical number, relating to balance in the Celestial realms. It has also a spiritual significance in Soul attainment. Thus, ten squared become 100—every realm of a Soul's experience must be squared before the 10 can be cubed. The squaring is the purifying and harmonizing of the attributes and potencies; the cubing is the perfecting of experience within the new realm. Thus also the four separate 1,000's, speak of the Four Kingdoms to be attained.

7 Then the fourth Degree bears the Soul into the Eternal. The River gains in depth, till even an Angel cannot take a Soul through it. Each one must learn to swim in it, and even to become a great swimmer. By this is meant, Soul attainment through entering into and accomplishing these Degrees. The High Initiate is thus enabled to *tread* the Waters. There is perfect buoyancy amid the Great Deep.

8 "This Mystery of GOD" indicates the profundity of the Message contained in the Vision. How few understand the Mystery of GOD. Apart from noble elect ones, every interpretation of Life, Man, the World, the Sun, and the Stars, is personal, individual, and material. Yet to the few who do understand, who seek to live in the consciousness of *the All Present ONE*, and who are humble and reverent, life becomes the sublimest of gifts; man assumes the importance of a potential Son of GOD; the World ceases to be a globe of matter; the Sun becomes a Divine World whence Angels and even Archangels proceed in ministry; and the Stars take on the fashion of GOD, and are HIS own embodiments for Celestial Ministries.

9 The River issues from the Sanctuary of the Eternal and flows through a channel adorned with the Trees of the Garden of GOD. For these are of the Divine Mystery aspected to meet the needs of all Life. The fruits of the Trees are for meat; they are of the Divine Substance, and the Leaves or attributes are of the Everlasting, for they have the elements of Eternal Life within themselves.

The Waters shall at last find all Souls; and they shall yet heal all the hurt streams of the Earth.

And the Initiates shall learn of the Great Mysteries; for they shall sit upon its banks, and learn to seek within its Pools, even in En-gedi and En-eglaim—the Celestial and Divine Deeps. For in these Pools are the Great Fish—the Sublime Mysteries.

Let him who readeth, understand.

It came to pass as I sat in the midst of the Seventy Ancients of the House of Israel, that the hand of the Lord God of Israel was laid upon me.[1]

It was within the sixth year, and on the sixth month, and upon the fifth day, that the Vision broke within me.[2]

Before me stood the Lord in the likeness of the Sacred Flame. In appearance He was like Fire from His loins to His feet; and from His loins to His head His appearance was like ineffable Radiance whose light was the colour of pure amber.[3]

He laid His hand upon my head and drew me up out of the earth into His Heavens.[4]

There He opened my understanding and gave me in vision the history of the House of Israel, and of Ierusalem which at one time was the glory of the earth.

I looked through the Northern Gate of the City, and beheld an image which had been fashioned by the spirit of jealousy in those who had wrought great wrongs within Ierusalem; it had been placed at the northern entrance to the Sanctuary, and near the Altar where the Glory of the Lord, the God of Israel, abode.[5]

[1] The Seventy Ancients of the House of Israel were the Elders. They were the Chief Shepherds and Teachers in Israel, those who at another period in their history asked that the Messenger Moses might veil the glory of his countenance when he came to them from the Divine Presence. To sit in their midst on the part of the Prophet unveils his relationship to them as the Messenger of the LORD. For the Divine Message had to be communicated unto the House of Israel through the Elders. The Messenger spake to the few, and these mediated it unto the many.

[2] These figures of years, months and days relate to the illuminations and ascensions of the Soul, and are connected with initiations and degrees of Celestial estate. It was after six days that the Master took on to the Mount of Transfiguration, Peter, James and John.

[3] Here is indicated the LORD as the Living Flame. The intensity of the Divine motion made the Presence appear as a Fire. The magnetic effect of the ETERNAL ONE in motion up and down the Spiral of the Divine Kingdom, or that of the Solar World, or even that of a world such as this, must be tremendous. Thus the appearance of fire. But the vision is entirely inward. It is Soulic. It is seen upon the Celestial and Divine realms. And it is beheld interiorly. A Soul can see the Lord of Love only when that one is recognizing from the Centre of the Being. For then that which is being realized is seen.

[4] The Spiritual Household of the whole earth was glorious. Of Ierusalem it is foretold that after her deliverance and redemption, she should have restored to her "the former glory."

[5] The Northern Gate of the City is the door or entrance of the magnetic realm. It represents the Mind in the individual and Planetary system. It is in the mind that most betrayals take place. In a fallen state it becomes the seat of pride and arrogance, the theatre of all kinds of exhibitions begotten of jealousy. There idols are fashioned and worshipped, for in bondage to evil states the mind becomes an idolator.

Then in the outer court of the Sanctuary I beheld how the wall had been breached to make a door other than that which belonged to the Sanctuary; and when I looked through the door, I beheld all the Ancients of Israel.

Each one carried his censer in his hand, and the cloud of incense rose unto the Heavens.[6]

The spirit of jealousy is the influence that led to great Planetary disasters. It was the cause of more than one potentate of the Celestial regnancies going out from the Divine Presence to seek another kingdom and found new dynasties. It led to the Betrayal of this Planetary Household. It brought down Lucifer and the one-time glorious Angelic Heavens of the Planet. It has lain behind, and been the leading factor in, the titanic conflicts in the Solar System, which resulted in the destruction of the Planes of the Planet, and such changes in the Solar Body that the Photosphere had to be formed as a veil and defence to the Sun's interior Planes and Kingdoms, and at the same time to be a vehicle through which to minister amid the changed conditions.

The spirit of jealousy set up the image of itself to be worshipped, and placed it inside the northern door of the Sanctuary and near the Altar where the overshadowing Cloud abode. When the spirit of jealousy finds an entrance into the Mind, it also subtly strives to gain dominion of the Sanctuary or Soul itself. It would displace the Shekinah also and have sole regnancy where alone the LORD PRESENCE should dwell.

This was the tragedy that overtook Lucifer and other members of the Planetary Hierarchy, and which brought down the once most glorious Ierusalem, making of its radiant day, a night of intense darkness.

[6] This is an astonishing passage. It is a vision of the actual state of "the Middle Kingdom" and the conditions amid which the Household of Israel lived and served. The breach in the Wall was the opening to his vision of the Astral Kingdom which was beneath but adjacent to the magnetic realms. In the Human soul system the Astral realm is beneath, in state, the magnetic realms, and related intimately to the Body. Whilst it is in the higher magnetic realms that the spirit of jealousy has its seat and sets up its image, the astro-occult sphere is where the greater number of the graven images were fashioned, and where they ruled over the children of men.

In relation to these things the Prophet beheld the seventy Elders of Israel. Amid the frightful conditions these still worshipped. They strove to commune with the Heavens and offer their prayers, represented as Incense. Though the conditions around them were appalling, yet the Heavens received the

But around them I beheld many things of evil which had been generated by those who had set up the image of jealousy to be worshipped instead of the Lord whose Glory was within the Sanctuary.[7]

These generations were all portrayed upon the wall that was around the court. They were beasts of evil form and desire, ravenous and destructive, and full of the venom of jealousy.[8]

Incense of their aspirations. It was something that they were able to retain their censers and offer their devotions.

[7] Here there is a cryptic reference to the effect of the Sodomic period. At that time the partially restored Heavens were denizened by evil images, magnetic and powerful, which were begotten of the states and actions of the Children of Judah when these became the vehicles of the betraying spirits who made their lives a record of sensual and lascivious conduct.

To worship these graven images was to love the life they called to, and make of religious emotion and experience a superfine sensualism. Such was done in many lands, as the records of history and mythical stories testify. Egypt, Greece, and Rome bear witness to this. So do many parts of Bible Story.

[8] The children of evil desire were magnetic and were actual living forms, fluidic and potent. Just as the intense desires of the Human Mind and heart, and the action resulting from these, write their signs and forms on the human Magnetic Plane, so does the racial conduct impress its results upon the Planetary Magnetic Plane. Thus the world's history was written upon the first Magnetic Plane that was destroyed at the period known as the Deluge. With the destruction of that Plane, the records were lost. The like thing happened to the second Magnetic Plane. This was balanced in two sections; one encompassed the Atmospheres of the Planet, and the other half was the Girdle or Bow in the Heavens. This latter was for balance and magnetic recovery. The history written upon the half that encompassed the Atmospheres was largely of the nature of Sodom and Gomorrah. That history was of a nature that cannot be written of in particular, but it formed the book of Sodom and Gomorrah. As such it became the afflicter of the Children of both Judah and Israel. And it caused to be repeated through great ages, the acts and states of the Sodomites.

The awful states obtaining, and the images with their magnetic action, had to be destroyed and the effects of their action blotted out. It was to do this that the Sin-offering was projected. And the work of the Oblation was the great redeeming work wrought out by the Divine Love called "the Passion of our LORD," in the accomplishment of which "the handwritings" on the Magnetic Plane were blotted out, and Redemption for the Race made possible.

Then the Presence who had upborne me to the place of vision said, 'Behold the darkness caused by the spirit of jealousy! In the midst of it all, the Ancients of Israel had to dwell for many generations.'[9]

The
Mystery
of
Tammuz

Then the spirit bore me to the Northern Gate and bade me look in the Sanctuary. And I beheld many who were as women weeping for their beloved; for Tammuz was dead. The spirit in the image of jealousy had slain him. So the Ancients of Israel mourned for him.[1]

Then the spirit brought me to the inner court of the House of the Lord.[2]

⁹ The above revealing will give indication of all that the Household of Israel must have suffered at the hands of the enemy through the children of Judah.

¹ Tammuz is the name of the Sun God. He was a mythological character in ancient Babylonia corresponding to the Greek Adonis. He was spoken of as "the Son of Life" and came to be related to Spring in the re-birth of nature. His death and resurrection were perennial. It was like mourning and weeping for the passing of the time of natural fertility, and rejoicing at his rebirth with the coming of Spring. Like Persephone, he descended into the bowels of the Earth and then rose again.

The mythological aspects are found in many lands. Yet the real meaning does not seem to have dawned upon interpreters. The name is associated with *sorrow*, and the anniversary became a festival of weeping. But in the true Hebrew Mysteries which were held by ancient Israel, Tammuz was the Angel of the Sun.

In a comparative sense he was ADONAI.

With this understanding of the inner significance of the Myth, the meaning becomes clear. To find Tammuz was to have realization of the ADONAI. To worship Tammuz was to recognize and adore the LORD of all Life. To mourn over Tammuz because of the loss of Him, was to signify that the consciousness and vision of ADONAI within the Soul's Sanctuary had departed, so that the LORD of Life was to the Soul as if HE were dead.

Who were they who had once known the LORD of Life and worshipped HIM? The Elders of Israel.

Who were they who could weep as women weeping for their lost-beloved ones, over the loss of ADONAI? The Elders of Israel.

How came it to pass that for them ADONAI was as one slain? Because the Spirit of Jealousy had destroyed in them the power to realize HIM.

It was the inward effect of the Great Betrayal upon the Elders of Israel, and consequently upon the whole Household.

² The innermost court of the Sanctuary was where the high Altar stood with its overshadowing Shekinah. It was the Court or the dwelling-place of the Cloud of Radiance and the Ark of Testimony. Within it was the Mercy-Seat—the Oblatory, and overshadowing it were the Cherubim. It was the Most Sacred House.

And when I entered by the door of the Sanctuary which was between the North porch and the Altar, I beheld five and twenty men turn their back upon the Altar of the Lord and His overshadowing Glory, though they confessed to having come from the East, and were worshippers of the Sun.[3]

And the Presence spake unto me, saying, 'O, Son of Man! It is no light thing that hath been wrought against the household of Judah; for those who set up the image of jealousy have in very deed filled the land with every kind of abomination, and made the Children of Judah commit in anger deeds of violence; and the spirit in the image of jealousy hath caused ignominy to be heaped upon the Branch of the Lord.'[4]

This has a Planetary significance, though it has also a Human application. In the Human Soul estate there is the inner Court of the Temple as well as the middle and outer Courts. In the innermost Court there are present all those elements of the Sanctuary which speak of the Divine Presence. There are the Ark of Testimony, the Oblatory, the Cherubim, the Shekinah and the Host. And in the Planetary constitution we have these same Mysteries cosmically expressed.

³ This is a revelation indeed! The door referred to is that of the Understanding. It is between the North Porch—the Higher Mind—and the Altar. The Prophet entered into the understanding of the effect of the Betrayal even upon the Planetary Hierarchy.

The Twenty-five Men represented the Twenty-four Members of the Occult Hierarchy and the one who presided over them.

It is a vision of what happened to the administrators of the Middle Kingdom when once the Betrayal had been fully effected. They turned themselves away from the Divine Presence when they permitted the Betrayers to influence them to carry out their wishes rather than the Divine Purpose. They do not merely turn their backs to the Altar of GOD. That in itself might have been for Divine Service; for there are various mediations at the Altar. There is service before it in the Soul's own act of devotion and worship. There is mediation through it in the offering of the Eucharist and Mass. But there is also mediation from it by the true Priest as he interpretates the Divine Will and gives the Blessing of the FATHER-MOTHER.

The Members of the Hierarchy were from the Orient. They had been sent by the Divine World to share in the work of the Planetary Evolution, and they were from the Sun and were worshippers of ADONAI.

⁴ The Branch of the LORD is the Christhood. The term is sometimes used in relation to a special Messenger. It is at times applied to the ADONAI. But it is always predicated of the Christhood.

The ignominy heaped upon The Branch was the humiliation of the Ancient Christhood. Its full manifestation was brought to an end. The Holy City of Zion was laid low. The real

And as I witnessed all the evil that had been wrought, and the number of the Souls who had been slain by the abominations caused by the spirit of jealousy, I felt as if I alone lived of all the House of Israel; and I fell before the Presence as one overwhelmed, and cried, 'O my Lord, the God of Israel! Save from these abominations the tribes of Ancient Israel!'[5]

Diaspora was not only the scattering of the Christhood communities of Ancient Israel, but it was also the humiliation of their powers.

Thus both the House of Judah and the House of Israel were smitten by the tragedy wrought by the enemy upon the Planetary Heavens; and even the members of the Hierarchy were so changed that they became heavily involved in the spiritual débâcle.

[5] How full of deep significance is the Prophet's prayer for Israel! He had witnessed in vision the effect of the Betrayal upon Judah and the Hierarchy, and he beheld how the Branch had been covered with ignominy and shame. Hence his prayer that all the Tribes of Ancient Israel might yet find deliverance and Salvation from the awful conditions that obtained.

The
Prince of
Tyrus

The Word of the Lord came to me concerning the Prince of Tyrus: [1]

'O Prince of Tyrus, why hast thou lifted up thine heart and laid claim to be as God, reigning in the midst of the Seas as if thou wert God? [2]

Though thou hast set thy heart to be even as God, yet art thou now less than the Son of Man. [3]

[1] The Prince of Tyrus was a Celestial Potentate. As the Text indicates, he stood in high esteem. He was not in estate the equal of the Planetary Angel, Ya-akob-El, nor were his responsibilities so great as those of the Angel Lucifer who was chief administrator of the Planet's outer Planes; yet he held the reins of the Middle Kingdom now known as the occult world.

At his command were many elemental powers and substances and many of those who ministered through these. As Prince of Tyrus he is said to have aided King Solomon to build the House of the LORD and the Glorious Temple, by providing wood, gold, gems, and workmen.

All these things belong to Divine Masonic Mysteries though they have been thought of and believed in as belonging to outer history. They were and they are Planetary and Solar.

The name Hiram is of Divine Significance, and is related to Ra and Ramah in its inner sense.

[2] Was it possible for such an exalted one to fall? Is not perfection found in such high estate? Is there no security anywhere against possible fall? These quite natural questions thrust themselves upon the mind, and they may even fill the Heart with dismay.

Archangels and Angels, Potentates Solar and Planetary, are immune from any such disaster through living consciously in the Presence of the Eternal Mystery Who is LORD of All. Such falls as are indicated in the Text, rarely take place. It is not often a Potentate goes out from that Presence and becomes apart, losing his Divine status and regnancy. And it is not to be thought of as eternal loss. If there were so, one who went out could never return. When such a rare event happens to disturb the Celestial or Angelic ministries, immediate action is taken with a view to restoration of the balance and the recovery of the Potentate or world that has gone out. The real cause of the Fall, and of all Falls, is here clearly indicated. It was pride of Mind and Heart, the desire to be great, to have dominion, and to be accounted as a God.

[3] The Fall of the Prince of Tyrus was so great that for the duration of his absence in his consciousness and state from the Divine Presence, he became less than the Son of Man as that estate is realized by one of the Sons of GOD. For the Son of Man relates to the individualized realization of EL ADONAI.

Behold how in thy day thou wast wiser than many. No secret was hidden from thee which could bring unto thine understanding the Wisdom of God.

Thou wast enriched with the Silver and Gold of the Treasure-House of God, and many secret things were revealed unto thee.[4]

In thy manifestation thou wast made the sum of Divine Beauty; there was sealed within thee the Wisdom of God.[5]

In the Garden of Eden thou didst walk with Wisdom, and all her precious gems were bestowed upon thee.[6]

The glory of them was thy covering: the Ruby and Sardius, the Topaz and Emerald, the Sapphire and the Amethyst reflected the Radiance of God unto thee.[7]

The Divine Workmanship of all thy qualities accomplished these things for thee in the day when God created thee.

Thou wast anointed of God, one whom the Cherub covered, to be set upon the mountain of God where thou didst walk up and down amid the Sacred Fire.[8]

⁴ For the work to be accomplished by means of the Middle Kingdom, Divine enrichment was absolutely necessary. The Silver and Gold of the Divine Treasure-House relate to the mercurial powers contained within the elements of his kingdom, and the inherited and acquired perceptions and realizations of all that Divine Faith and Love imply, by the Prince himself. He had reached the height of Divinity wherein some of the greatest secrets could be made known unto him; for these were also necessary for the sublime work he had to do; for he had not only to administer his own kingdom, but, in so doing, also provide Solomon with the wherewithal to build his Sacred House of Prayer and Service. That Sacred House was the Temple of Christhood.

⁵ How exalted his estate was, is herein revealed. For to be the sum of Divine Beauty was to be such an embodiment as would transmit the Glory of GOD as that Glory could be revealed within a Planetary Household. He was clad in the garments of a Planetary Divine Potentate, and arrayed in auric splendour. The Wisdom of GOD in relation to his own Celestial System was his inheritance. The Seal of the GOD of Ya-akob-El was upon him.

⁶ The Garden of Eden was the Garden of the Gods where great ones walked in the Divine Consciousness in the same degree, in which experience it is said they "walked with GOD." To have had the capacity to be the Head of the Middle Kingdom, implies Celestial Sonship to GOD.

⁷ The Precious Gems signify Divine Qualities. All Divine Qualities, though said to be gifted from the ETERNAL ONE, are attainments. Their possession indicates the path trod by the inheritor and the high degrees he has taken in the Divine Schools of the Mysteries. The Prince of Tyrus had for his covering the qualities of the Sacred Tinctures represented by the Ruby, Sardius, Topaz, Emerald, Sapphire, and Amethyst—representing Life, Counsel, Wisdom, Love, Devotion, Balance. These qualities enabled him to receive the reflections of the Radiance of the Eternal as the Divine Glory was magnetically poured forth from the Divine World.

⁸ Here may be glimpsed the Mystery of a higher order of Soul evolution. In every Human Soul there are latent the potential attributes of a Son of GOD. It is difficult even for those mystic

Thou wast perfect in thy ways from the day of thy manifestation until thou didst go out from the Kingdom that was given unto thee, and from the overshadowing Presence, and so didst fall from thy first estate which was bestowed upon thee within the Garden of God.[9]

Because of the wisdom that was in thee, and all the treasures thou didst possess which were of the Secrets of God, thou didst wield power within the Kingdom appointed unto thee, and thy regnancy gave joy to the Sons of God.

The Kingdom given unto thee was radiant, for the Glory of God filled it.'[1]

*   *   *   *   *

'O Prince of Tyrus!   Behold now the state of the Kingdom that was thine to reign within and administer!

Behold how thy wisdom and thy riches have been changed and become as false knowledge and merchandise![2]

Souls who once knew many of the Divine Secrets, now to realize the estate they themselves then enjoyed; for the conditions obtaining in this world militate against such a realization. But if such realizations could again be theirs, they would then understand this seeming reference to a yet higher order of evolution than is cognized upon these planes. For even the Sons of GOD who came to this Earth as its Light-bearers had a different history from that associated with the creation growth and evolution of the children of the Planet. For the Sons of GOD who came here were the House of Israel; but the children of the Planet were of the House of Judah.

The Prince of Tyrus was overshadowed by a Cherub. He enjoyed that degree of the glorious Mystery. He was energized by the Sacred Fire.

[9] There is something of glory here; then pathos; then tragedy. It is so strange that Biblical Scholars and commentators should have failed to discern anything here beyond the glory and fall of an earthly Prince whose chief rule was over one comparatively small city upon the shores of the Mediterranean. They do not appear to surmise even in the least degree that there was anything Cosmic in the description of Tyrus and its Prince. Yet the description is that related to a Son of the Gods who was perfect in the way of his manifestation until something happened to him that changed his estate and caused him to go out from the Divine Presence.

[1] That his regnancy gave joy to the Sons of GOD, lifts the veil to the Cosmic character of the ministry of these latter, and their relationship to the several Hierarchies and their appointed Heads. In these was an intimate relationship between them and Ya-akob-El, the Angel of the Planet, Lucifer, the Angel of the Outer Sphere of the Planet, and the Prince of Tyrus, the one regnant over the Middle Kingdom. As this latter Kingdom had an important part to play in the Ascensions of the Planet's Children as the Sons of GOD ministered to them, the perfect administration of it rejoiced them. For in its circuli they found the Divine Radiance reflected in the measure that was necessary for the perfect accomplishment of their own mission.

[2] It is a dramatic and pathetic appeal. The fall of his Kingdom was through his own fall. The materialization of Wisdom veiled the inner vision and gave a false interpretation of the Mysteries of GOD. The wealth of attribute and potency which had always

From the radiance of the Heavens thou hast descended into the great darkness!

From the heights of the mountain of God thou hast fallen into the depths where the discord and violence of evil are made manifest.[3]

Thou knowest no more the joy of the covering Cherub, nor the Glory of God's Overshadowing; for, since thy great betrayal to go out from His Presence Who created and fashioned thee, thou has been a dweller amid the iniquities of those who left their first estate, and who have made of the Holy City of Ierusalem a place where the destroying arrow flieth and the terror doth hold sway.

Thou who didst possess the power that is bestowed from on High by the Highest, art now humbled in the sight of all who should have beheld thy radiance and thy beauty, but who look in vain into the Kingdom where thou didst once reign gloriously, for the revealing of God.[4]

O Prince of Tyrus! though thou hast fallen so far from thy heavenly estate, yet will I Who am thy Lord, cause My Fire to burn within thee, and make all the evil done within thy Kingdom to be consumed away until not even the ashes of the evil remain.

And in that day shall all those who went out with thee also return, and be filled with astonishment at all that I shall cause to be done for thee and for them.'[5]

been related to the Giver of All, had lost its primal meaning through the Prince in his fall associating all such with his own individual aggrandizement.

³ It is like the flight of that one who is spoken of as the Fallen Angel. From the exceeding Brightness of the Magnetic Glory of his Kingdom he descended in his state into conditions that brought about the great darkness where discord crept in and led to deeds of evil and even of Planetary violence. For there followed this sad descent, those titanic battles of mythology within the elemental kingdoms which resulted in disaster to the Planet's upper elemental kingdoms, and then to its planes. For it became a conflict of the elementals in which the Gods became more and more involved; for more than one member of this system suffered most grievously through the Earth's tragedy. It eventuated in a conflict between good and evil, the Light of Divine Radiance and the outer darkness, Obedience to the Divine Magnetic Laws and the will of those who sought to fix the magnetic pole of all elements and make a materialized world with immovable planes and phenomena.

⁴ This is at once an indictment and a lament. It is an indictment of those who brought about the fall of the Hierarchy of the Middle Kingdom, and with these the whole of the Planet's Kingdoms; and it is a Divine Lament over the loss of the Prince of Tyrus. For he had been a glorious Son of the Gods, and one held in high regard by the Celestial Hierarchy. And the Divine sorrow over the loss of the Middle Kingdom in its once radiant magnetic state, was immeasurable, for it had become the dwelling place of those who betrayed the Prince and deceived the Angel Lucifer and the seat of their dynasty and throne of their regnancy, from whence they smote all the children of the Planet and wrought grievous things against the Sons of GOD.

⁵ That such a Divine Lament should be followed by such a promise is another testimony to the Love of the FATHER-MOTHER. For it implied the hope of the Heavens that all the Hierarchy would be restored to their former estate and regnancy; and also that all who went out from the Divine Presence in the great Planetary débâcle would not only be recovered, but in the accomplishment of it would stand amazed at the work wrought out for them and the Planet. Here the Divine Passion in the Oblation is anticipated.

A
Description
of
Ancient
Tyrus

The Word of the Lord came to me when I was dwelling within the City that had been laid waste, even Ierusalem, sorrowing that the Holy City had become so desolated of all that once it had stood for, and that it had now to bear the reproach heaped upon it by those who were strangers to it because they knew not the beauty and the glory with which its Sanctuaries and Palaces were filled before the day in which it also shared in the fall of the Prince of Tyrus.[1]

And the Word of the Lord said unto me,

'Son of Man; hear thou how the Heavens lament over the fall of the Prince of Tyrus, and the City of his one-time glorious reign.[2]

O City, that art situated at the entrance to the Great Sea, the venue for the Souls of many Isles in their search for the riches of Wisdom![3]

[1] The laying waste of the Holy City, which has generally been related to the little Palestinian City, was the destruction of the Planes, Palaces and Sanctuaries of this World, known in the Heavens as Ierusalem of Judah. For the Planes that fell under the ban of the enemies who brought about their materialization and fixity, were the elemental powers which encompassed the Planet, and which were the media through which the generation of forms of life took place.

The Palaces were the many mansions or spiritual states or degrees of Soul experience into which Souls entered and dwelt from time to time as they made their spiritual pilgrimage represented by growth and evolution of attribute and consciousness.

The Sanctuaries were those spiritual Households of mediation where Angelic Love and Wisdom were interpreted by the Christ Souls who had been sent to this World to minister unto its children.

Ierusalem shared in the fall of the Prince of Tyrus, which was the fall of the Middle Kingdom, as will presently be unveiled.

[2] For the Heavens to witness the Fall of one of its Princes and the realm of his regnancy, must be an overwhelming event to many. To speak of the Lament of the Heavens may seem a contradiction of the belief generally entertained concerning Life upon the Heavens; for the idea obtains that there sorrow is unknown. But most people confound things that are essentially different; for it is possible to have grief on behalf of others and yet know no sorrow such as is the resultant of our own pain and sense of loss. The sorrow associated with the Earth-life is absent from the Heavens; but Divine Grief can be experienced.

How one has longed through these latter years that the Churches through their Priests, Bishops and Popes could hear the Divine Lament over this world and all its children, and learn the reality of the Divine Grief over the Fig-Tree that bears little more than leaves, and the Vine whose grapes are rare—the Church that should have borne the fruit of the Divine Love and Wisdom.

[3] The City of most ancient Tyre or Tyrus, was situated in the magnetic circulus of the Planet. It was on the borders of the great Astral Sea—the great deep of the Planetary circuli. It was above the Astral Kingdom but operated into it and through it. It was that realm which in later ages has come to be

In thy beauty thou wert perfect, even as thy Prince. Those who built thee perfected thy form; and they placed thy borders in the midst of the Great Sea.[4]

Thy vessels of transit were all built out of the Fir-trees of Senir; their uprights were fashioned out of the Cedars of Lebanon.[5]

Bashan formed for thee thy powers of transit, out of the Oak-trees beneath which the sacrifices were offered;[6]

associated with the Occult Kingdom. It was compassed by the magnetic belt. In the Human constitution there is the correspondence in the higher Mind or Intellect.

It was the Middle Kingdom where many aspects of Planetary government were carried out, and where Souls acquired their first knowledge of the Mysteries. Those who ministered there held many of the Secrets of the Celestial World, called great riches; for these were the riches of Divine Wisdom which were communicated to Initiates of the various Isles or Spiritual States.

⁴ The Magnetic World was perfect; the glory of the Angelic Kingdom was reflected into it. It was therefore full of Angelic beauty and light. The Zidonian part of it was adjacent to the Angelic World. In the unfallen days the Angels were able to visit both Zidonia and Tyrus, and give prolonged ministries. In the Angelic World direction the borders extended into the midst of the Ætheric Sea. For it was through those realms that the Solar Body rendered its ministry.

⁵ The vessels of transit were the mystical and occult vehicles or elemental powers.

The Fir trees of Senir were the evergreen or abiding spiritual elements out of which Life itself is built up. For Senir is of Mount Hermon where the Dews of God rest upon the tender roots and leaves, and its Majestic Fir trees or Eternal Substance built up the forms that were as musical instruments giving forth songs of praise.

The uprights or standards were of the Cedars of Lebanon; for the standards relate to Righteousness, and such stately masts of a Planetary Argosy are of the substance of the Cedars of Lebanon or the Christhood.

⁶ The Oak Trees of Bashan signify fruition, and the offering up of the fruits in Sacrifice.

There can be no true spiritual transit from state to state except by means of Sacrifice of all the powers of the Being. This is true not only of an individual Soul, but likewise of a Planetary Soul. The Oak tree is not only the symbol of strength and endurance, but also of the very Kingdom over which the Prince of Tyrus held regnancy. After the Fall was fully accomplished the God of the Tyreans was Baal. The Mystery deepens; the fall of Tyrus

THE MESSAGE OF EZEKIEL

And the companies of the Asshurites formed thy canopies from the sacred woods of Chittim: Egypt supplied thee with fine linen which had been beautifully embroidered, that thine uprights might be able to respond to the Breaths like the sails of a ship to the Winds.[7]

From the Isles of Elishah were given the Blue and the Purple coverings which are in service in the Sanctuaries of the Lord.[8]

Those who served as mariners within the Argosy of thy Kingdom were of ancient Zidon and Arvad; and thy Pilots were all of those who knew the Isles of the Great Sea, and had gathered in of their riches of beauty and wisdom.[9]

was the descent in state of the Magnetic Kingdom, embracing
the whole of the occult world and its Hierarchy. There are
indications in the Old Scriptures that the worship of Baal under
the Oak Tree and the offering of sacrifice, were echoes of earlier
ages when the truth was known concerning the City and Prince
of Tyrus.

[7] The Asshurites were the elemental spirits in an unfallen
state, beautiful in service because obedient to the Divine Law.
They had a ministry of guardianship, and so are said to have
fashioned canopies from the Cypress Wood which has an inner
meaning relating to the Eternal Youth of the Soul.

Egypt represents the sphere of the outer vehicle; and also the
land of earthly wisdom. The beautifully embroidered fine
linen is nothing less than the beautiful attainments of the Soul,
without which it could not catch the Breath wafted to it from the
four dimensions. The sails upon our uprights must be the fine
linen of the Saints. A true empiricism gives power of motion.
We are borne by the Breaths according to the degree of our
wind-receivers. Our sails clothe our uprights in the measure
in which we grow.

All this was true of Ancient Tyrus.

[8] The Isles amid the Great Sea represent spiritual states and
estates or attainments. The Soul in its growth and ascensions
passes from Isle to Isle within GOD's Great Deep. The Isles of
Elishah relate to the more advanced attainments wherein are
the deeper experiences.

Elishah was the son of Javan. They are both Divine Names.
The dwellers on those Isles were the sons of Eli-sha-yah. There-
fore they had the inheritance represented by the Blue and Purple
Coverings. These latter were related to the Sanctuaries in the
Angelic World. They were the coverings of the Altars, and
formed the veils between the inner courts.

In the Planetary sense the giving of these coverings to the
City of Tyrus unveils momentarily the office of the Sons of GOD
in their ministries unto the Prince of Tyrus.

[9] The metaphor is very beautiful in the allegorical description
of the Middle Kingdom. The whole realm is as a ship upon the
Great Deep full of precious treasures, captained by a Divine

The Ancients of Gebal strengthened thee by unifying thine elements; they came in their Argosy upon the Great Sea with their servants and riches.[1]

In thy hosts were found Ancients of Persia, Lud and Phut; these adorned thy walls with their insignia and coverings, and added to the sum of thy beauty.[2]

Potentate and staffed by Sons of GOD who were of ancient Zidonia, the Home of the Mysteries, and had passed through the land of upper Arvad, or the higher pilgrimage.

The Pilots knew the Isles of the Deep. In their education in the Divine Mysteries, they had passed that way and gathered in of the wealth of the Divine Love and Wisdom.

[1] Gebal means a mountain of GOD. The Ancients of Gebal were, therefore, of the Divine Kingdom, and must have come from the Solar Body; for they had the power to unify all the Elements of the Middle Kingdom. They did not belong to the Argosy of Tyrus, for they came in their own Argosy across the Great Deep. Their ministry revealed the inter-relationship between the Solar World and this Planetary Household.

[2] Persia, Lud and Phut, though names of persons and lands, were also mystical terms. Persia was of the Ancients or the Christhood. It was the land of the Christhood ministry. Cyrus was its Prince. The term Cyrus is the Persian for Christ. It is synonymous with Christos, and possesses something of the quality of Kurios, the LORD.

Lud was the son of Shem who was the son of Noah the builder of the Ark of the Soul. The name therefore is related to the Divine. He was the progenitor of the Lydians who dwelt in Asia Minor. But this latter signifies the minor degrees of the realization of the Spirit, as Asia itself in the larger sense signified the more universal ministries of the Spirit. The Seven Churches addressed by EL ADONAI were communities of the Christhood in the land or state of the Spirit—Asia. Phut was the son of Ham, and therefore was related to the Divine World originally. The Lydians were said to be his descendants. The name signified the Wisdom that is of Egypt, or that which comes to the Soul through the lower degrees expressed in the objective realms of manifestation.

Amid the hosts of Tyrus who dwelt and ministered there, were descendants of the Sons of GOD operating within three different spheres. They all wore their original covering or garments, and were distinguished by their celestial insignia. The effects of their ministries were manifest upon the Elements which in their formative motion were designated "the Walls."

The dwellers in Arvad sentinelled thy walls, and those of Gammadim thy watch-towers: they ministered of thy comeliness and made manifest thy perfection.[3]

But all this greatness hath been lost, for those who directed thy Argosy brought thee into strange waters. They caused thee to be lost amid the Great Sea.'[4]

[3] Those who were of the great Pilgrimage—Arvad—sentinelled the walls; they were watchers of and sharers in the work of the Occult Kingdom; and the Gammadim were its defence; for these latter were as buttresses like Knights of the Gates.

[4] Herein we find a description of the Earth's Tragedy. The Great City of Tyrus was brought low. The directing of the Argosy into strange waters lifts the veil that hid from human gaze the treachery by which the Planet was changed in its course and all its Kingdom thrown out of harmony. Those who came to this Earth to found a new dynasty caused the downfall, through descent of state, of those who had the control of the magnetic streams of the Planetary Body. They intercepted the messages signalled from the Divine Kingdom, and gave a version of these which was a negation of the Divine Purpose. In response to what they thought was a Divine command, those who had the direction of the Planet's magnetic streams caused it to move away from the Plane of the Divine Ecliptic, and gradually to settle down into a world whose Planes became fixed.

That was the beginning of this World's tragedy. It was once a glorious Body in the Celestial Heavens, the true Emerald Isle of the Great Sea. It was as an emerald set amidst the Stars; for its Sacred Tincture was Emerald, and its glory like that seen amid the great sea of Crystal around the Throne of the Eternal.

Again the Word of the Lord came unto me, and I was commanded to set my vision towards Zidon, and declare unto that land the purpose of the Lord, the God of Israel.[1]

Behold, O Zidon! Thus saith the Lord God: 'I will be glorified within thy borders and in the midst of thee; and thy people shall come to know Me as their Lord Whose judgments are holy and not after the manner of those who judge unjustly and without mercy. For they shall be sanctified when My Presence is a Dweller in the midst of them.[2]

In that day there shall be no more any cause of pestilence within thy borders, nor those who defile thy land, nor those slain by their evil ways.[3]

[1] In the Old Testament Scriptures Zidon is associated with Tyre, and they are coupled together in a saying attributed to the Master wherein it is reported that He said that in the day of judgment it would be more tolerable for Tyre and Zidon than for Capernaum and Bethsaida.

Nor is this seeming relationship accidental. For in the Ancient Mysteries they stood adjacent to each other. In one Path of the Soul's growth and evolution it passed through the land or kingdom of Tyre and then that of Zidonia. Tyre was the occult or higher intellectual aspect of the Mysteries; Zidonia was the realm where their spiritual significances were gained. It belonged to the upper circulus of the magnetic realm.

Those who governed that Celestial Province of the Planet were well versed in Celestial Lore. They were related to those who were spoken of in later ages as the Gods of the Phœnicians. For these were members of the Solar System. In the fallen days it thus came to pass that the profound knowledges of the Celestial and Planetary Kingdoms found remarkable reflection in the inner and outer history of the Phœnicians.

The fallen state of Zidonia through the betrayal of her Princes, interfered with the mediation of the Angelic World, deflected the Messages sent to the Zidonians, and changed the meaning. Thus the inner meaning of the Mysteries became lost.

[2] The Divine Purpose is declared anew. The Divine World had set in operation those ministries which it was hoped would ultimately restore Zidon to its original estate. Its Princes were to be reclaimed and the ancient glory of their regnancy once more made manifest. To understand the Divine Mysteries through realizing them is to glorify GOD. No Soul could know HIS realization and fail to radiate something of HIS Wisdom unto the Tyrean Borders of the Soul's Kingdom; HIS glory would then shine. And as of the individual, so of the Planet. The Kingdom of Zidonia and that of Tyre must again reveal HIS glory.

[3] There is reference here to the misuse of the Mysteries. The Pestilence within the borders was the degradation of those things which were and ever are essentially spiritual. The influence of the Sodomic evil had penetrated as far as Zidonia. The Life forces were put to uses which were out of harmony with Divine Law. Rites and ceremonies were introduced which act upon

And thou shalt be no more as a thorn to pierce the side of My people, the Ancients of Israel; nor shalt thou harbour those who have despised Me, and rejected those who came from Me to perform My Will in the midst of thee.[4]

For, when I shall have gathered all Israel out of the midst of the peoples amongst whom they have been scattered, and they once more become sanctified for My Service, then they shall dwell again in thy land which I gave unto My Servant Ja-acob-El to rule over, and they shall work in My Vineyard without hindrance or fear, and know that I am in their midst as in the ancient times.'[5]

the spiritual nature like a pestilence acts upon the outer body. The Home of the Celestial Mysteries thus became the circus of grotesque impure revelries. The true Celestial Pantheon of Zidonia where the fellowship of the Gods was enjoyed, was turned into a Temple where sacrifices were offered unto strange gods. The conduct of many Zidonians hurt even the Angelic Kingdom to such an extent that its adjacent circles had to be changed.

What it was necessary to effect throws light upon the preceding reference to the Divine Purpose, and it incidentally reveals the stupendous nature of the task undertaken when the Oblation was projected.

[4] This is an illumining passage in relation to the spiritual history of Israel upon this Planet; for it shows by inference the sources of much of their burden-bearing. The fall of the Kingdom of Zidonia as well as that of Tyrus was not only a tremendous blow struck at the work they had come to accomplish, but it caused those two kingdoms to become theatres of dramatic and often even tragic opposition to their way of life. The fallen Zidonians even more than the fallen Tyreans, were as a thorn in the flesh of Ancient Israel. By their age-long inimical attitude and activities they prevented the recovery of the Planetary Household. And where the Tyrean and Zidonian are found to-day in unredeemed state, the Sons of GOD find it difficult to make manifest the Christhood, and effectively serve unto the accomplishment of the Redemption of the Planet's children.

[5] As the result of the accomplishment of the Oblation, this is now to be fully realized. Many of the Sons of GOD are entering anew into the consciousness of their LORD's Presence.

The
Mystery
of the
Pharaoh

The Word of the Lord came to me and commanded that I should speak unto the Pharaoh of the Egyptians, and to all his hosts.[1]

'O Pharaoh! Unto whom dost thou liken thyself? Who hath made thee great?[2]

Behold, now, the Assyrian! He was once a Cedar in Lebanon.[3]

[1] The Pharaoh of the Exodus is associated with Cruelty towards the Children of Israel. Yet the name is of Divine origin. It is a remarkable confirmation of this origin that the Biblical Scholars of our own time relate the origin of the name to the early Hebrews, that it then became Arabic and Greek. That the name was not Egyptian though given to an Egyptian Monarch, and that its origin was Hebrew, bears out the mystical significance of it, and also of the history with which it is associated.

The name signifies a Royal Estate, and has relation to the House of Light. Even the Great Pyramid of Ghizeh was so called.

The Pharaoh, to distinguish him from the many who in the outer Egypt took the name, was one of the Princes who were appointed over the land of Egypt, mystically understood. That is not only the land of generation, but the kingdom wherein the Soul learns much Wisdom out of Earth's experiences. The outer manifestation represents a realm whose ministry is educational. Within it by observation, relating and correlating, the Wisdom of the Egyptians becomes the Soul's heritage.

In a Planetary sense the Land of Egypt was the unfallen Astral Kingdom, which was adjacent to but lower than the realm of the Prince of Tyrus, who was the regnant head of the Occult Kingdom. It had its Mystical Delta through which the sacred river flowed, whose waters then emptied themselves into the Great Sea or Deep. For the Delta of Lower and Outer Egypt had originally seven branches; and these mystically represented the seven nerve centres of the Body into and through which the most Sacred Magnetic Lifestream flowed.

The Pharaoh of Egypt had, therefore, a most important Kingdom to rule over. But when the Princes of Zidonia and Tyrus *fell from their first-estate*, the Pharaoh also became affected and fell.

[2] Here is indicated the nature of his fall. He became high and lifted up in the pride of his heart and thought himself a God amongst the Gods.

[3] The Assyrian was once a Cedar in Lebanon. Who was he? To be a Cedar of Lebanon is to be of the Christhood. Was he one of the Sons of GOD? These are natural and pertinent questions.

Historically the Assyrian was of the ancient Babylonia. On the Earth-planes he belonged to a high civilization. If the

His great branches were beautiful, for he dwelt beneath the overshadowing Cloud.[4]

Of great stature was he; he reached into the Cloud of the Glory of the Heavens.[5]

The waters of God nourished him in the midst of the Great Deep, out from whose bosom came he forth to be set up on high.[6]

The streams from on high enriched his roots, as they flowed amongst the trees in the land that was his heritage.

He grew, until in height he overtopped all the other trees of the land; and he extended his branches until he became a cover for many.[7]

Babylonian Gods were many, originally they were all of the Angelic
and Celestial realms. To find vestiges of the originals in the
Earthly Babylonia postulated that those who founded that
Ancient Kingdom knew the Angelic and Celestial Hierarchies.

In the Human Soul estate the Assyrian represents the Mind
in its Divine Nobility; in the Planetary Estate the Assyrian was a
Celestial Potentate. His sphere was within the realm of the
Magnetic Circuli; his regnancy was administrative unto those
who had for their office the generation of the manifold forms of
the kingdoms of the outer manifestation.

⁴ His attributes were beautiful as became a Celestial Son of
GOD. These were his Branches. He dwelt beneath the Overshadowing Cloud, which, in a Planetary sense, is of great significance.

⁵ As the representative of the Celestial Mind of the Planet he
reached great heights in his estate. He was like one dependent
from the overshadowing Heavens. The glory of the Planet's
Mind was reflected in and through him.

⁶ The Divine Elements are represented by the waters of GOD.
In the midst of the Eternal Mystery of the Great Deep, he was
prepared for his special responsible mission. He was sent forth
out of the Great Deep as that was related to this system to col-
laborate with the Princes of Zidonia, Tyrus, and Egypt in the
work of Planetary evolution under the administration of Ya-
akob-El.

⁷ He had access to the Divine magnetic radiations which proceeded from the Divine World, and these established him in his
kingdom through nourishing his potencies. All the Trees were of
Celestial estate in relation to this world. They were the members
of the Hierarchy who ministered within the Assyrian's Realm. He
was their Prince. He had grown in Celestial estate until he had
risen above his brethren in the stature of spiritual potency and
attribute, until by virtue of his estate he was chosen to be prince
of the Hierarchy whose members were to administer many of the
Elements in the generation of forms. As he himself was overshadowed from the Divine World through the Celestial Realm,
so was he to be as an overshadowing presence unto many. The
Planetary Mind would be as an Azure Vault beneath which
many forms would come into manifestation.

His boughs were used as resting-places by all the birds of the Heavens; beneath them the creatures found protection and by them the people knew themselves overshadowed.[8]

Thus was he beautiful in his greatness; his glory was not hidden by the other trees in the Garden of God; nor did any of them envy him.[9]

*   *   *   *   *

Consider this, O Pharaoh of Egypt! Why hast thou desired to lift up thyself to the height of that Assyrian, and to spread forth thy branches like his?

To whom dost thou liken thyself in greatness and glory amongst all the trees in the Garden of God?[1]

⁸ There is given here a glimpse of the unfallen conditions of life upon this Planet, and how the tender-mercies of the Divine Love and Wisdom were over all HIS Works. The creatures were at home beneath the overshadowing. Those were days before the night fell upon all the Planes of the World.

How beautiful was Life then in the Planet's manifestation! The world was young indeed in its spirals and motion. Alas! that it should have known such a change from Light to darkness, from harmony to discord, from perfect trust to awful fear and dread.

⁹ The Assyrian was beautiful in his greatness. He was a lowly yet majestic son of the Gods. In the Garden of GOD he was great in Estate above all the other Sons of the Gods who had been sent to minister; yet there was no spirit of envy in these latter that he should occupy such an exalted, royal regnancy and be crowned a Prince amongst the Planetary Gods.

¹ There is something most touching in the Divine appeal. Let the reader try to imagine what it must have meant to the Divine World to witness the descent of the several minor Gods who had been appointed unto the Government of this world: the Betrayer took first one and then another from their high estate wherein, as the appointed Potentates, they reigned for the Divine FATHER-MOTHER. The same temptation ensnared them all.

The Betrayers worked upon them the same evil that overtook themselves, and led them to forsake the Divine Law of creative manifestation and go out from the Divine Presence through descending in their estate.

The Betrayers caused to be changed a communication from the Divine World sent through the Planetary Angel Ya-akob-El, to Lucifer the Angel of the Seventh Sphere, and thus brought the whole Planetary Cosmic exposition of the Divine Love and Wisdom down in its state. Then the Betrayers affected in turn each of the Potentates who were at the head of the various departments and spheres of ministry. They insinuated the very spirit which had caused them to fall from their high estate—the spirit of pride of place and power. Thus self-exaltation and arrogance became manifest in all they did.

It was this influence that overcame Lucifer after he had been

Behold, now, that which overtook the Assyrian in the day of his exaltation when he was in the fulness of his greatness and beauty!

The enemy came upon him and threw him down; he was laid low, so his glory departed.

No more can the people dwell beneath his overshadowing branches, nor the creatures find protection, nor the birds of the Heavens resting-places.

The breaths of hell smote all his powers and bore them down unto the nether land.[2]

betrayed by the false message. Then there followed the Prince of Tyrus, the Princes of Zidonia, and the Pharaoh of Egypt.

[2] Here is a description of the fall of the Prince of Ancient Babylonia. The spiritual estate of Babylonia was high and great. It was a spiritual civilization higher than the manifestations of Life within the land of the Pharaoh or the outer Body of Manifestation, Planetary and Soulic. It was a Kingdom ruled over by one who was the Chief Prince of Zidonia—the home of the Mysteries. It was the intermediary spiritual sphere into which the Mysteries were communicated from the Divine World in signs and symbols, and where the higher Initiates were initiated into Planetary Mysteries. Souls had to pass through this sphere ere they could reach the Celestial Lodges or spheres wherein the Solar Mysteries were unveiled.

It was also the sphere from which the ministrants who were manifestors and interpreters in the realm of the Prince of Tyrus, received the Mysteries translated into the tongue of that sphere— or the language of Signs and Symbols accommodated to the occult or higher intellectual realm.

This further glimpse will reveal the importance of the realm over which the one named the Assyrian presided. And it will indicate how great the descent was which overtook the Assyrian and all his Babylonia.

The Mystery deepens and the significance increases in the knowledge that Ancient Babylonia was a Solar Mystery.

The Glory of any Soul, Human, Planetary or Solar, is dependent upon the realization of the Divine Presence. To go out from that Presence brings realization to an end. As in the realization all the magnetic potencies are affected from the Divine World and caused to pour forth radiations, so in the degree in which realization is lost is the decrease in potency and radiance. Hence the loss of glory that came to the Assyrian.

With that departure of power, his regnancy became weakened. No more was he as the Head of Gold or the overshadowing golden radiance within the Angelic Kingdom of the Planet. No longer was he able to make his realm one full of sure resting-places for the soul-pilgrims on their way to the Divine. Nor was he in a position any longer to give counsel unto the Pharaoh of Egypt concerning the realms of manifestation. The breaths of hell had smitten him. Now hell signifies confusion, disorder and darkness.

Great was the mourning for him: the Great Deep, out from whose bosom he came, was sorely troubled because of him; the motion of its waters had to be stayed by the Hand of God.

Lebanon mourned for him in the day of his hurt; and all the Cedars of Lebanon were smitten in his fall.

Those who had grown up with him within the Eden of God went down into the darkness of hell and knew its pains and sorrows. They became like those who are slain.

All the peoples were shaken by the commotion caused by his fall; for he took them with him in his descent into the abyss.

When he went down into the fearsome pit which the enemy had dug for him, he and all who were with him became overwhelmed in the darkness, amid which they were made to pass through the consuming fires of the nether-world, and bear travail unspeakable.[3]

The Nether-world is the Hadean World, or the land where the magnetic light shines not. Hell is within it; and the Tartarean World is the place of penal fires or the realm of purgatorial ministries within Hell itself and the dark spheres.

[3] The Sorrow of the Heavens over all who went out was most real. The whole of the Great Deep or Ætheric Sea by which the entire system is encompassed, was sorely moved. When a world changes its polarity and motion the whole of that Sea is affected, and all the members which move within that Sea become afflicted. So great was the disturbance caused by the change in the Earth's conditions, that only by the action of the Divine World was the Earth saved. The magnetic disturbance had to be stayed by the Hand of GOD.

Lebanon mourned for him and all who went down; because Lebanon is the Divine Kingdom, and all the Sons of GOD upon that Kingdom were dismayed at what had taken place. Even the place or state of the Sun had to be changed, and all the Cedars of Lebanon were smitten. These latter were the members of the Christhood.

Those who had grown up with him in the Eden of GOD, were related to members of the Hierarchy and administrators within his Kingdom. These all went down into the darkness, or the Great Night which overtook the world; and through long ages they have had to suffer pain and anguish in their travail as they have striven to recover themselves.

With the descent of such a Great One, all the people or children of the Planet became affected. The ages bear witness to this. All the races have suffered much and the elder races most, because they had most to lose. Next came the children of this Planet known in ancient times as the Children of the Adoption, for these were robbed of the power of Life represented by the first degrees of Jesushood. After these came the Ancient Christhood or Sons of GOD, who had been sent to this world for purposes of manifestation and ministry. The degree of their suffering has been unspeakable. They have travailed in their endeavour to retain the Divine Flame and Radiance, and to be faithful and loyal unto their LORD. Nor have most of the members of the Hierarchy been lacking in great burden-bearing as they have served, whilst the Divine World has laboured to bring back the lost world to a state of spiritual equilibrium of its Planes and Divine Polarity through the restoration of its deflected Poles.

Since the day of his going down, the Lord God of Israel has very specially had to minister unto all who were of the Cedars of Lebanon, and those who had been in Eden, the Garden of God, to comfort them in their travail with Waters of Life from the streams which flow through the Garden of God.[4]

O Pharaoh of Egypt!   When the Assyrian was exalted to the Heavens, thou didst also share in his exaltation; but in his fall thou fellest also.

From ruling over a land of rich streams of light and wisdom, thou didst pass to become the ruler of a country amid arid sands desolated with great deserts where the fires of desire burn those who travel across thy highways, and where captivity and oppression are known.

Such is the state of the Pharaoh of Egypt to-day.[5]

And with thy descent, O Pharaoh of Egypt, many of the great ones who were the Nobles of the Earth, went down into the nether-parts, drawn down by those who drew thee down into the abyss.[6]

[4] Herein there is a world of Revelation. It indicates the very special provision that had to be made for the members of the Hierarchy and the Christhood. Rare ministries had to be given by the Sun and Moon, the former to the Hierarchy and the Sons of GOD, the latter to the Planet itself.

The streams from the Garden of GOD were magnetic. Amid the greatly impoverished planes and elements the Sons of GOD suffered terribly. But the Divine Love found a way to convey nourishment to them. Even in recent ages the Sons of GOD within this Planetary System have had special Solar ministry accorded to them. The magnetic streams sent to them they breathe into and through their spiritual body. Indeed, this world cannot supply them with the necessary spiritual sustenance to enable them to remain here and minister. So the Divine World does it direct. They get little more upon this Planet than the elements of nourishment for their outer vehicle.

[5] The Pharaoh shared in the power and joy of the exaltation of the Assyrian, just as the outer life of any Soul shares in the blessing of the inner. And *vice versa*. If the spiritual world within a Soul becomes veiled, and the power to live in the heights of conscious spiritual vision and purpose is gradually enfeebled, so will the land and life of the outer manifestation become involved, and share in the loss. And as this is true of the Soul, so was it and still is it, true of the Planet. The outer shares the inner, whether it be predicated of Planet or individual Soul.

The outer planes of the World to-day testify of this. They are as the arid sands and scorched deserts which speak of the awful disaster which befell the magnetic Plane great ages ago.

[6] The fall of the Pharaoh meant the descent of the world in all its outer manifestation. There were many noble ones upon the Earth, Souls who had attained to considerable powers of administration under the guidance of the Sons of GOD. The ruling of these latter was purely theocratic, for the LORD was their King, and HE administered unto them as a community, by means of an oligarchy formed of those who had been in high office ere coming to this world. These Sons of GOD appointed those who were to serve in the capacity of rulers and administrators in the more outward affairs of life. These nobles went down in the great descent. Elsewhere, what happened in the nether world will be unveiled.

Though thou wert surpassingly beautiful, the enemy caused thee to dwell amidst those who fell from their first high estate.[7]

Asshur is amongst the slain of the Nobles of the Earth. She fell into the pit that had been dug, and found her grave there.[8]

Elam accompanied Asshur. Her Ancients were drawn down and found themselves betrayed ere they knew it, to be enclosed in the prison-houses of the nether-world.[9]

Meshech and Tubal are also there. The enemy overcame them in their warfare with the titanic elemental forces, and cast them into the abyss where the terror had its dwelling. [1]

[7] That implies that the Pharaoh became such as those Angels who left their first-estate became. This is set forth in the History of Israel in Egypt. For even in relation to the outer Kingdom he made manifest the spirit of oppression and even cruelty. He made his dwelling with those who caused this once most beautiful Earth to become the land of oppression, pain and sorrow.

[8] Asshur belonged to Ancient Babylonia. On the outer planes it is supposed to have been the capital. Its mystical significance was, therefore, great. It was the realm of the operation of special elemental forces. In the unfallen days, these elementals had a great ministry to render. When the betrayal had been fully accomplished, and the various kingdoms fully affected through the changed magnetic status of the Planet, all the elemental spirits went down in their state. Owing to the greatness of their power and magnetic motion, they wrought most grievous hurt within all the Kingdoms of the Planet.

There is deep meaning in the Scripture that reads:—"Asshur cannot save us." For it refers to the elementals who had so fallen that they could no longer fulfil the mission on which they were sent.

[9] Elam accompanied Asshur. The Elamites were of the Ancients. These latter were of the Christhood. Many of the Sons of GOD were drawn down even into the Saurian Hells; for they followed those children of Judah who left the true Human Kingdom to minister to them and bring them back. Ere they realized what was happening, they found themselves in prison-houses prepared by those who left their first estate and betrayed this world. Some of the vestiges of those awful prison-houses still remain.

[1] Meshech and Tubal are also there. These are likewise representative names of elemental powers, like the chariots and horsemen of Egypt. They had the ministry of causing the magnetic streams to flow into the outer spheres, and bearing these to the various avenues of service.

That they were cast into the abyss where the terror reigned signifies the greatness of the change that overtook them. For the terror that reigned was the frightful resultant of the mis-directed elemental forces in the various Kingdoms, producing discord, disorder and spiritual loss.

The dwellers of Edom are all there, the kings and princes of the land; they were slain by the sword of the great enemy who fashioned the abyss and laid snares for the elect of the land.[2]

Zidon was even brought down.   Her princes were slain. The Terror overwhelmed them.[3]

O Tyrus!   O Zidon!   O Egypt!   what a time of sorrow when ye went down!   And what the travail has since been![4]

No one could imagine what the conflicts between the various elemental spirits accomplished when misdirection was given to them as the result of the changed polarity of the Planet and all the elements in the various Kingdoms. The battles were titanic.

² Edom was the land of forgetfulness, understood mystically. To go down into Edom was to lose Soul-remembrance. It was to forget the Soul's heritage and ancestry.

In a Planetary sense it was the Kingdom of Esau. He sold his inheritance for a mess of pottage. He represented the Earth-side of Ya-akob-El's Kingdom after the fall. He represented also the nomadic spirit that is a wanderer, ever restless, seeking satisfaction in the fallen state of the elements.

The enmity between him and Ya-akob is an allegorical presentation of the conflicts in the Middle Kingdom and the great fear of ultimate loss that beset Ya-akob. With the Pharaoh went down all the reigning powers of the land.

³ Zidon has already been explained as the Home of the Mysteries. When her Princes were slain, mystically, there came to those who knew the Mysteries, the loss of interior knowledge through the veiling of the Intuition. These Princes were the true Masters or Rabbis of the Celestial Masonic Lodges. In their descent, by the operation of Divine Law, they ceased to hold the secrets.

⁴ How deeply moving this lament is! It is the cry of the Divine World over the loss of the Angelic, the Middle and the Lower Kingdoms of this Planet. And though many efforts have been made to recover the loss by means of Solar as well as special Angelic ministry, yet it is only now that the Planet has taken the upward arc in its spiritual life which will ultimate in its perfect recovery and restoration. And this upward and Godward motion is the outcome of the Oblation, or Sin-offering as it has been called, issuing in Divine Atonement for individual Souls and the Planet. And Atonement is nothing less than perfect oneness with and in the Divine.

What the Travail through the ages has been, no man could even imagine. And the Travail of the Oblation was an up-gathering of all the ages concentrated into the burden of the Divine Passion of the Oblation, of which the Soul known as Jesus Christ was the vehicle.

A Vista
of the
Oblation

Then I was let down to the planes where dwelt those who were of the Captivity; and I sat me down with them for seven days, full of astonishment at all I had beheld and heard.[1]

And the hand of the Lord touched me and bade me arise and look out upon the planes; and I saw there what I had beheld when I was carried up of the Spirit.[2]

And the Vision overwhelmed me, and I bowed myself unto Him whose Presence stood before me.

Then in my spirit He caught me up, so that I again stood upright before Him.[3]

And He said unto me, 'Son of Man, when thou goest, thou shalt shut thyself within thy House.[4]

[1] The whole of this part of the Prophecy as found in the Text of Ezekiel is so changed in presentation that it would be utterly impossible for any translator to give a correct rendering. This passage has suffered more than many of the other parts of the Book. As will be shown in these "Notes," the Logia relate to the Oblation.

The Prophet was overwhelmed by the revelations given to him concerning the Betrayers, the Betrayal, and the Betrayed. For the captivity was not a merely outward bondage of Judah and Israel; it was racial and Planetary, and it even reached cosmic dimensions. In the Prophecy the Betrayers are clearly indicated, when once the Mystery of the Fall is unveiled. No wonder he was overwhelmed. Few who have read his Message have even vaguely dreamt of the stupendous nature of the Betrayal and its ramifications.

[2] Here is indicated a repetition of the vision of the Cosmic tragedy. When carried up of the Spirit he witnessed the transcendent vision of the ETERNAL ONE, and had given to him the consciousness of the state of the Planet-Soul and all her children, and the condition of the whole House of Israel amid the débâcle. When he was let down to the Planes of the Planet— that is, in his consciousness and vision—and looked out upon them, he had painful confirmation of all he had seen.

[3] Readers will note how often the Presence is referred to, and how important the part that is played by His influence upon the Prophet's vision. Without the Presence, he is nothing. The Presence and the Spirit are one; and it is within his own Spirit that he is affected. His visions are not mental pictures. They are not the products of the occult world though later he has to look into that world. His visions are the children of his Soul's vision, and of the varying degrees of his realizations. Without the Presence he could not have endured; without the power of His Spirit he could not have witnessed the Divine Drama nor the Solar Cosmic Tragedy.

[4] Elsewhere the meaning of the expression, "Son of Man, when thou goest," will become obvious; for it has relation to his call and the Mission to be undertaken bye and bye.

"Thou shalt shut thyself within thy House" has prophetic reference to the Great Silence which befell the Christ-Soul

*And thou shalt lay siege against the enemies of Ierusalem;
for they encompass it and besiege it.*[5]

*In the conquest of the City, thou shalt take upon thy left
side the burden of Israel; for upon thy heart must thou bear
the iniquity of Israel until the enemy be overthrown and the
fulness of days be accomplished.*[6]

when the Oblation had to be undertaken, and during the ages of
its duration. He was shut up within his house. During the
period of his ministry in the wilderness amid the wild beasts
and the satanic influences which had fashioned the wilderness
and its states, the Christ-Soul was unseen by and unknown to
his Brethren. None of his Brethren could imagine what that
strange seclusion and silence meant to him.

⁵ The Ierusalem referred to here was the whole Spiritual
Household of the Planet and not the little city in Palestine.
The Ierusalem beneath was at one time like the City of that name
which was above. It represented a state of pure and beautiful
communal life. As the Above so was the Beneath in its degree.
  But Ierusalem had fallen. It had been brought low by the
enemies of the LORD of Love. These enemies encompassed it.
They had besieged it for long ages. They filled the Planetary
Heavens. They were the powers by which in high places, evil
principalities had been set up. They had made of those Heavens
which were once the scene of Angelic Ministry, a wall that shut
out the Angelic Heavens. Upon the wall were featured every
kind of evil thing. These were the graven images which were
the grotesque masques of everything pure, true and lovely.
They had been established upon "the middle kingdom." They
were the hand-writings which had to be destroyed and blotted
out. To these the Prophet was to lay siege. He was to attack
them unto their overthrow. For this tremendous Planetary
work only one who was in the state implied in the terms "Son
of Man," could have become the vehicle of the Divine World.

⁶ This and the three following verses contain most remarkable
illumination upon the Sin-offering and Oblation. The mighty
work had to be accomplished by the Divine Love, first for Israel
and then for Judah. The Son of Man, Oblator and Redeemer
for the LORD of Love, had to lie upon his left side as he bore the
iniquity of Israel. For this action signified the travail of Love—
the Heart—on behalf of Israel. And it was to be endured until
the enemies of Israel who had caused the iniquity should be
overthrown and the purpose of the Divine Love be accomplished
in Israel's deliverance—"in the fulness of days."
  The travail of the Redeemer as Israel's Daysman has been the
age-long burden-bearing of Love. The purification of the

And upon thy right side must thou take the burden of the iniquity of Judah, and bear it for forty days, until the iniquity of Judah be purged away.[7]

Behold! I have appointed each day.[8]

And until thou hast ended the days of the Siege, and accomplished the conquest of the City, I must put bands (limitations) upon thee, saith the Lord God of Israel, to guard thee.'[9]

Planetary Heavens through the blotting-out of the graven images, was essential to the recovery and restoration of Israel. For even the Elders could not fully rise into the Angelic Heavens until the Oblation was fully accomplished.

⁷ The burden of the iniquity of Judah was to be borne for forty days, even until it was carried away. During the process, "the Son of Man" as the Oblator, was to lie all the time on his right side.

The right-side symbolizes centrifugal force, a majestic display of force, the welding of the sword of truth. It speaks of the conflict he would have with the awful powers and principalities that dominated the Heavens of the Planet, and the sacrificial ministry necessary for the overthrow of the manifold evil states.

⁸ The forty days or periods were the forty lives which were necessary for the Oblation. The Son of Man, as that saying had relation to the Master, spent forty lives within the Planes of this world in the very special ministry of being the Burden-bearer for Israel and Judah. They were the forty lives in the Wilderness. Each Life had its portion appointed. The Master was the vehicle of the Divine Love; in each Life the travail of the Divine Passion was beyond telling. Even here there is no particular information given. Nor was there in the Gethsemane. The nature of each Life's ministry had to be veiled from all curious gaze, and even from the Angels who desired to see into the Mystery.

⁹ Here is a revealing of the real Humiliation of "the Son of Man." The powers of Christhood in him were to be, as it were, tied up. Bands or limitations had to be imposed upon him. Shut up within his own House and thus limited, he would be guarded from the evil machinations of those who would gladly have destroyed him. In order to enable him to accomplish the Work, he had even to be guarded from himself. Had the powers of Christhood been operative during the Oblation he could not have wrought many of the works that were necessary for the overthrow of the powers of evil; nor could he have endured the awful sorrow and anguish that would have been his in all the Lives, and very specially in some, had he had the Christ power to look within and remember.

*To the
Shepherds
of
Israel*

The Word of the Lord came unto me and commanded that I should speak unto the Shepherds of Israel. And I spake as the Spirit gave me utterance.[1]

O Shepherds of Israel! Thus saith the Lord God unto you:—

'The woe of the unfaithful has fallen upon you. Of you it has been said that ye eat the riches of the Love and Wisdom of your Lord, yet forget to nourish those who have been impoverished.

The reproach concerning you is that ye have not healed those who have been wounded, nor bound up the broken and maimed, neither have ye strengthened those who have been weakened in the way.

It is even said of you that ye have scattered the sheep and made them easy prey unto the enemy whose emissaries are as ravenous beasts; for the sheep have been without true Shepherds.[2]

O Shepherds of Israel! Why has it come to pass that the enemy of My Flock should find you unguarded as if forgetful of your heritage from your Lord, and your service unto Him?[3]

[1] When the Word of the LORD comes to a Prophet, it is not only the Message that is implied: the Word is the Divine Presence. Nor is it that Presence only in the general sense in which the Holy ONE comes to every Soul who realizes the Divine. It signifies a very special approach of ADONAI. This approach is by means of the Cherubim and Seraphim. The Divine Elemental World becomes the vehicle of the magnetic streams which flow unto and into the Prophet from the ETERNAL. The Prophet of such standing is the recipient of direct ministry out from the midst of the Four Dimensions. The Ætheria through which the Divine Message is communicated, is itself of the Eternal Mystery, and is the very Substance or Flesh of ADONAI. Therefore, the vibrations which result from the passage of the magnetic rays through the Ætheria or Divine Substance, convey the Message.

Whilst this is proceeding, many minister unto the Prophet, for he has not only to be sustained amid the tremendous play of Divine Magnetic forces, but he has also to be guarded.

The effect of the Divine outflow unto him, and the influx of magnetic energy, is to give the Prophet a deep consciousness of the indwelling Spirit, and the power to respond to the Spirit's motion.

[2] There were many Orders of Shepherdhood in Israel. In a general sense they were all Shepherds; for they were teachers, interpreters, leaders and guides of the people. They were a band of the Sons of GOD. In the Great Planetary débâcle resulting from the betrayal, they all suffered in their shepherdhood; for their powers became impoverished. They had been greatly smitten when the woe of the unfaithful befell them. They had been recognized by the sheep or children of this World, as those who had been very specially gifted and privileged, through the knowledge of the Divine Love and Wisdom; but with the loss of their powers through the effects upon them of the prevailing conditions, they had become as those who had proved themselves unfaithful to the mission on which they were sent. They had lost the power to shepherd Souls. Those who should have been Divine Therapeuts had lost the Divine genius to heal.

[3] Here we pass from the general to the particular. Amongst the Band of Shepherds who represented the Divine Cosmic Shepherdhood unto this Planet in its unfallen days, there were many who occupied the position of chief Shepherd or Elder.

Behold, saith your Lord! I will search for My sheep until I find them, though they be scattered abroad.

Even as an earthly shepherd seeketh out his flock and gathereth together those that have been scattered, so will I find all My sheep; for I will deliver them out of the hands of the enemy, and bring them back out of the land of darkness.

And I will restore them to the land of Israel, and bring them back into My Pastures; and upon the slopes of the Mountain of God they shall become once more My Flock, and one Fold.[4]

The Flock refers to the whole of the Tribes of Israel. They were the Sheep of the primary Fold of GOD upon this Earth. They were those lost sheep referred to by the Master whom He came "to seek and to save." There were other sheep also whom He had to find, but Israel stood first.

The enemy spoken of referred not only to the prevailing condition of life, but rather and very specially to those who set out to destroy the Christhood manifestation and ministry. The sad and hurtful condition might have been transcended by Israel but for the persistent persecution on the part of those who had left the Divine Kingdom, and who were opposed to this World becoming a perfect spiritual system.

It was not easy for Israel to remember their Divine Heritage and the service on which they had been sent. And the Divine Chiding is unto those who had belonged to the more inward branches of ministry, who were of the House of I-O-Seph, whose special ministry had been, and should have been always, that of priestly Shepherds unto the greater House of Israel.

[4] *The great diaspora* had taken place ages before the time of the Prophet. The real Israel had been effectively scattered by the enemy. There were to be found of the vast company of Souls who left the Heavens of their own System to come to this world to teach and shepherd its children, only small groups of Souls scattered over the various lands. There were many absolutely lonely ones whom no man accounted of regard, to whom this world with its strange life was like a nightmare dream: it was so full of conditions that gave poignant pain and anguish, whilst it also seemed strangely unreal. To most of Israel this world has been such for ages; but at different periods members of different tribes were able to make an appearance in the lands whither the Prophets, Seers and Messengers were sent. It was thus during the period covered by the ministry of the Messengers I-O-Seph and Moses, and also during the time covered by the major Prophets.

That was the reason why the Messages of the Messengers and the Prophets were addressed in a special manner unto Israel.

To gather Israel together one more, redeemed from the land of bondage, healed of all wandering, rejuvenated of the Spirit, and regenerated in all potencies and attributes, was the sum of all the true prophetic utterances, and the living Message of the LORD, the GOD of Sabaoth and LORD of Israel.

And I will give them a Shepherd who will lead them, even David, My Servant, the Beloved one. And he shall be as a Prince of God amongst them, who will, in the Name of the Lord, drive out of the land the beasts of prey that have wrought evil.[5]

He will gather again the Shepherds of Israel unto the high places of blessing upon My Holy Mountain where the rains of the Heavens will lighten upon them.[6]

As the Trees of God in His Garden they will again flourish and bear fruitage; even unto the earthly parts shall come the blessing increasingly.[7]

They shall know hunger no more as in the land of their bondage, nor the shame which the oppressors heaped upon them; for the Glory of their Lord shall be upon them, and they will become renowned as His Shepherds.

And it shall be made manifest that the Lord God of Sabaoth is with them.'[8]

[5] The term David had much more than a merely personal significance. According to data David had been removed to higher spheres. The term could have been used to express an idealized state. It means The Beloved. In the prophetic vision it refers to Him who was sent as the Manifestor and Redeemer. As the Manifestor He would become the Shepherd appointed to lead Israel back: as the Redeemer He would be the Servant of the LORD and the vehicle of HIS Passion for the overthrow of all the evil states obtaining in the Middle Kingdom, and the destruction of the magnetic beasts of prey. In the Manifestation he would have to give those Teachings which would attract Israel as green pastures the sheep; in the Redemption He would have to carry the burden of the Oblation. And He was of the House of David in that He was a Beloved One who was appointed to represent the BELOVED OF ALL.

[6] The Elders of Israel were to be gathered first. This was the Work the Master was sent to do. He had first of all to find those who were His immediate Brethren. He Himself was of the House of I-O-Seph. To find members belonging to that House was His constant desire. He looked out for them. It was to the few of that House whom He found in the Days of the Manifestation, He unveiled the Mystery of the Oblation. With rare exceptions, all His intimate friends belonged to that innermost House of Israel. They were to be found and brought back to the high places of the land of Israel. These latter were the Altar Stations upon the Spiritual Heavens with their correspondences within the Soul. They were all to rise again unto great altitudes of Divine Vision and realization in preparation for the work of World Redemption.

[7] They were the Cedars of Lebanon, the Christs of GOD. That was why unto them very specially, Christ was made manifest. The restoration of the Christhood Estate would regain for them the Beauty of Holiness, even to their earthly parts. Herein lay the promise of the Regeneration.

[8] The new Manifestation that is coming in these days is to be an embodiment of Jesus Christ in and through every Son of Israel. All Israel is to be saved. The recovery of Israel will be the arising of the Sons of GOD. They will arise out of the states of their sorrow and suffering to reveal anew that the LORD GOD of the Heavenly

The Lord laid His Hand upon me in blessing; and He bare me up in the motion of the Spirit.

And He opened my vision and revealed to me the state of the whole of the House of Israel.[9]

And He likewise made known unto me His Holy Purpose concerning Israel in the land of Judah.[1]

Hosts is with them. With such a consciousness in them they will regain the power to minister as The Shepherds of Israel, and become renowned once more as the manifestors of GOD.

⁹ This is a Cosmic Vision. It relates to the aeonial travail of the whole House of Israel amid the planes of Judah. It is dramatic in its situation and dioramic in its action. There are elements in it akin to the visions of the Gethsemane, though not to be measured with the ever deepening tragedy of the latter. Yet the two events were, and are, intimately related.

¹ 'Israel in the land of Judah' is an expression pregnant with vital meaning. We read of Israel in Egypt and Israel in Babylon, and these are considered to refer to years of captivity; but Israel in the land of Judah is not associated with any form of bondage.

Yet in spiritual Planetary history the expression relates to age-long captivity. For the House of Israel in the land of Judah means much more than might be gathered from the history of Israel as set forth in the Old Testament. In Jewish sacred literature, Israel and Judah were just two Kingdoms of one people. For a time they had separate Kings. There were times when the two Kingdoms were opposed to each other, and even entered into conflict. But the real Israel never belonged to the Jewish race. These latter were the children of Judah. They were the offspring of this world and belonged to one of the sub-races.

On the other hand, Israel represented a distinct people. The true Kingdom of Israel was not of this world. The real Kings of Israel were Solar. They were of the Gods. And HE who was King of all the Kings and LORD of them all, was the LORD GOD of Sabaoth. For the true Kingdom of Israel was a Theocracy.

The Land of Judah was something more than the parcel of land known as Palestine. Such designation came through a local application of the mystery of the Planet. The full Kingdom of Judah was the whole Planetary sphere of manifestation. Israel in the Land of Judah signified the presence of Israel for purposes of ministry in the midst of the Planetary life.

It was, therefore, in the Land of Judah that the sad captivity of Israel took place; and it was within the disrupted Kingdom of Judah, that *the Great Diaspora* of the House of Israel took place.

The Divine Holy Purpose concerning Israel, as will be shown, had to do with the redemption and restoration of all the Ancient

In my vision I beheld a valley peopled with the dead, as if a multitude had been slain in it, for the valley seemed to be full of the remains of the dead.

In the open champaign everything appeared to be very dry, as if the Breath of Life were absolutely absent.[2]

The Voice of the Presence spake to me saying, 'Son of Man, thinkest thou these dead can live again?'

And I answered, 'O my Lord, Thou Who art the Lord God of Israel alone knowest.'

Then was I instructed what to prophesy concerning the restoration of the whole House of Israel.

O ye dead within the valley of death, hear ye the Voice of the Lord your God; for thus speaketh He:—

'Behold! I will cause the Breath to blow through the valley, and ye shall live again.

I will clothe your bones with sinews, and your sinews with flesh, and your flesh with a covering; and will cause the Breath to fill you, and ye shall live and again know Me as your Lord.'[3]

Now as I prophesied, a great sound broke the stillness. It was the coming to life of those who had been dead. Bone came to bone in unity, and sinew to sinew, and the covering of all parts with flesh and skin.

Then did I hear the Voice speak to the Four Breaths, saying, 'Come now, O Breath, and breathe from the four quarters of the Heavens upon those who have been dead, that they may live again.'

And the Breath from the four dimensions moved within them and made them live again.

And they arose and stood upon their feet marshalled as Hosts of the Lord.[4]

Christhood—the Sons of GOD who came to this world or Land of Judah, to minister.

2 This vision was retrospective as well as of the then state of the House of Israel. The depth of sorrow and anguish revealed in the Vision, though unvoiced in the description, no one could gauge who had not been privileged to look through great ages and witness the spiritual wanderings of Israel and their descent into the valley of deep humiliation wherein they experienced the death of all their hope and vision. For conditions upon the Earth smote them cruelly, and oppressed them until the spirit of Life within them was utterly crushed. The path of their travail for long ages appears like a great valley of death, a place where the Breaths had not blown.

3 If the reader could have looked out upon the valley of the dead and witnessed all that the Prophet beheld, he would not have had much hope for Israel. For the one-time spiritual planes of the Planet had become a veritable wilderness of death. Indeed, there was a time when it was questionable whether it would be possible to rescue and restore this world and all her children within her Gates. Israel could have been taken away, but there was no other intermediary world to act as a dwelling place for the Children of Judah, and they could not have endured the vibrations and magnetic streams of the outer Solar spheres; for they had not grown sufficiently in their Soul estate. The Planet could have been restored through the action of the Solar world reducing the outer fixed planes. But that would have taken great ages to accomplish, and would have involved the loss of many races. In order to save the children of this world it became necessary for Israel to remain, even though life had to be lived and service rendered amid conditions that were as a valley of death.

The vibrant promise of restoration was, therefore, one calculated to fill Israel with new hope.

4 O LORD GOD! How can these dead live again? That which seems impossible even to a Prophet may be accomplished by the Divine Love and Wisdom. Long before the Divine Purpose could be fully realized, the Prophet witnessed an astounding miracle. As he prophesied, the broken attributes were made whole; the separated powers were brought together; the

Then spake the Voice unto me, saying, 'These are the whole House of Israel. And they say "Our very bones are lacking in marrow, and are dry; and our hope of Salvation has grown dim. We are as those who are put away."'⁵

Therefore, Son of Man, say unto them, 'Thus saith the Lord God of Hosts, O Israel My people, how cometh it to pass that ye have forgotten Me?

Behold, once more shall I come unto you, and the graves wherein ye were laid shall deliver you up, and the enemy who put you in them shall be overthrown;

For I shall again make My Name glorious in your midst.⁶

The Waters from the Fountain of Life will I pour out upon you, and ye shall be cleansed from the stain of the evil that overtook you.

The Heart will I again cause to beat in unison with My Will; for I will renew its substance.⁷

impoverished conditions gave place to enrichment; the leanness of the fashion was changed into spiritual robustness; the controlling centres were all restored; the spiral became again complete; and the Divine Defence ensphered and covered all the parts.

Then the Breaths moved from the Four Dimensions, passing over them and into them, giving new energy, re-empowering all the potencies for creative service, and crowning each life with regal dignity.

As a result, the Hosts of Ancient Israel stood up upon their feet, a mighty array of marshalled Sons of GOD for the service of Planetary Redemption.

The prophecy foreshadowed these times—the Latter Days. The sound breaking the great stillness followed by the mighty arising, is now proceeding. It is the effect of the Breaths which are blowing upon Israel from the Four Dimensions. And this Message is unto the whole House of Israel. It is the address of the Word of the LORD unto them.

[5] A pathetic touch, showing how far down Israel had gone in the long ages of travail. They often felt as if the very life-essences had been sapped from them. It is not easy to keep hope alive and faith undimmed in its vision, when all the conditions are like inimical waves dashing upon the shores of life.

[6] Here is the promise of a very real resurrected life. In that regained state, Israel will no more forget the LORD. It was a part of the cruel sufferings they had to endure that, owing to the dire nature of the elemental and racial conditions, they lost the memory of HIM whom once they most loved to serve.

Great is the tenderness of the Divine Love as HE chides them into remembrance.

[7] The Waters from the Fountain of Life are the magnetic streams from the Divine World. Through the Solar World, these are now being poured forth; for the Sun is the reservoir of the Eternal Waters of Life for this system. And in a most intense and very special ministry, these streams are now being poured out upon the Household of Israel.

These Streams will make the Divine Heart of every true Israelite beat in unison with tne Divine. In the Spiral of the Being there will be the perfect Systolic and Diastolic action of the innermost realms.

My Spirit once more will I cause to move within you, that ye may be upborne and able to walk before Me to fulfil My Statutes and learn anew My Secrets, and from henceforth dwell in the realm of My Presence, even the patriarchal land which was thine in the ancient times.[8]

And I will tabernacle in the midst of you; and the children of Judah shall come to know that the Lord God of Hosts is in the midst of Israel.

Thus shall I make manifest through Israel the Glory of My Name.'[9]

[8] For the HOLY ONE will then be able to move within the Sanctuary of the Being, up and down the Spiral, in the realization of which the Israelite shall once more come into the consciousness of the Presence of the LORD of Love, and understand again many of the Divine Secrets.

[9] The tabernacling in the midst of Israel is by means of the above experiences, for these make unto true manifestation. Through a noble manifestation of Life will the children of Judah, and other Souls who are just now on this Planet, be able to discern the Glory of GOD's Presence in the midst of Israel. It is through manifestation that Israel is to be the embodiment of the Son of GOD and thus to exalt the Divine Name; and also, to share in the Divine Travail unto the perfect healing of this world.

For the next Manifestation is not to be only cosmic in nature, message and service, and expressed through only one of the Sons of GOD, but is to be the restored Christhood of the Whole Household of Israel.

This is the first Resurrection, which the Prophet foresaw, and which to-day is being realized.

It will be a glorious finale to the long ages of travail.

MARANATHA.

INDEX

TO

"THE MESSAGE OF EZEKIEL"

★

Asterisks denote either definitive statements or statements of special note.

Also indicates a different tense of the word quoted.

See also indicates a related word or passage.

MEETINGS

Regular meetings are held, at which all seekers after the Divine way of life are welcome, in the Sanctuary at the Headquarters of the Order of the Cross, as below, every Sunday at 11 a.m. and Wednesday at 7 p.m. throughout the year (except during the Summer Vacation); and there are Groups or Reading Circles for the study of the Teachings in many provincial towns. Also in Australia, France, New Zealand and United States of America. Details will gladly be sent on request, in writing, to the Trustees, at the address given below.

COMMUNICATIONS

Communications regarding the Literature of the Order should be addressed, and remittances made payable to, "The Literature Secretary," The Order of the Cross, Snelsmore House, Newbury, Berkshire, RG16 9BG.

Further information concerning the Order of the Cross and its activities will be gladly given to any inquirer, on application to:

THE SECRETARY

THE ORDER OF THE CROSS

10 DE VERE GARDENS, KENSINGTON, LONDON, W8 5AE

SYNOPSIS OF MAIN PUBLICATIONS

THE MASTER sets forth the Inner Meanings of the Master's Teachings and gives a true picture of Him as He was in His Life, public and private. The Birth Stories and the Allegories of the Soul are revealed in their true setting; with the Teachings on the profound Mystery of the Sin-offering, and the Allegories of the Soul's Awakening.

THE LOGIA contains the chief utterances of the Master, in the form in which they were spoken by Him. Here they are restored, including the real Mystic Sayings, found in the Synoptic Records, the Gnostic Record, the Pauline Letters, and the Apocalypse, containing remarkable histories of the Soul, the Planet, the Ancient Christhood Order, and the Oblation or Sin-offering.

LIFE'S MYSTERIES UNVEILED gives the Path of Discipleship and Aids to the Path of the Realization. It includes definitions of terms in their relation to these Teachings and many answers to questions asked at Healing and other Meetings. The principal theme of the volume is Initiations of the Soul.

THE DIVINE RENAISSANCE: VOL. I. Concerning the Message of the Order of the Cross and the Messenger. The Seeker, Finder, Attainer. The Superstructure of Man; the Soul's Fashioning. The Mystery of Being. Worship and Prayer. The Nature of Evil. The Truth and how we may know it. The Authority for these Teachings. Revelation and Illumination. The Divine Purpose of the Oblation. The Redemption. The Mystery of the Mass. Altar symbolism.

THE DIVINE RENAISSANCE: VOL. II. Unto the Great Silence. Science and Religion. The Angelic Realms. Corpus Christi; Jesushood, Christhood, the Lord-consciousness. The Sabbath of the Lord. The Mystery of the Ascension. The Beginnings of Historical Christianity. The Advent of Paul. Apostolic Succession; Pentecost. The Church of the Living Christ. The Seven Sacraments. The Reformation; the need for a Renascent Redemption. Advent and the Mystery of the Seven Thunders. The Healer, Manifestor, Redeemer. The Divine Passion. The Obedience of Christ. Our Lord and Our Lady, the Feminine Aspect of Deity. The Three Altars. A Divine Oratorio. The Ministry of the Gods and Divine Government. Theocracy. The Mystery of Prayer. Cosmic Consciousness. The Regnancy of Christ.

THE MESSAGE OF EZEKIEL. *A COSMIC DRAMA*. The Office of a Prophet. The Purport of the Book. The Divine World Unveiled. The Distinction given to Israel. The Mystery of Tyre and Zidon. The Pharaoh of Egypt. The Arising of Israel. The *Logia* of the Prophet Ezekiel: with extensive Notes to the *Logia. The Logia of Israel.* Vol 1.

THE MYSTERY OF THE LIGHT WITHIN US. *With 17 coloured plates by Amy Wright Todd Ferrier*. i. The Luminous Cross and the Cross of the Elohim. ii. The Spectra of Souls and Stars. The Solar Fashion. iii. Auric Glimpses of the Master. iv. Celestial and Divine Estates. v. A Holy Convocation. Jacob's Ladder. The Adamic Race. The Secrets of God. The Girdle. The Blessing of Israel. A Divine Rhapsody.

ISAIAH. *A COSMIC AND MESSIANIC DRAMA*. i. The Unity of Divine Revelation. ii. The Prophecy. iii. The Word of the Lord. iv. A Divine Drama. v. The Mystery of the Sin-offering. vi. A Momentous Promise. vii. The Triumph of Adonai. viii. The Drama of Israel. ix. The Sign of the Cross. x. The Daysman of Israel. xi. The Appointed Redeemer. xii. The Five Cities of Egypt. xiii. The City of the Sun. xiv. The *Logia* of the Prophet Isaiah: with extensive Notes. *The Logia of Israel.* Vol. II.

PUBLICATIONS

By the REV. J. TODD FERRIER:

THE MASTER: *His Life and Teachings*	Large Crown 8vo	624 pp.
THE LOGIA: *or Sayings of The Master*	Large Crown 8vo	436 pp.
LIFE'S MYSTERIES UNVEILED	Large Crown 8vo	480 pp.
THE DIVINE RENAISSANCE, Vol. I	Large Crown 8vo	402 pp.
THE DIVINE RENAISSANCE, Vol. II	Large Crown 8vo	560 pp.
THE MESSAGE OF EZEKIEL: *A Cosmic Drama*	Large Crown 8vo	280 pp.
THE MESSAGE OF ISAIAH: *A Cosmic and Messianic Drama*	Large Crown 8vo	436 pp.
THE MYSTERY OF THE LIGHT WITHIN US With 17 plates.	Large Crown 4to	240 pp.
THE HERALD OF THE CROSS (Bound volumes) Vols. VIII upwards.	Large Crown 8vo	
GUIDE AND GLOSSARY INDEX	Demy 8vo	432 pp.
HANDBOOK OF EXTRACTS of the Teachings of The Order of the Cross, from the Writings of the Rev. J. Todd Ferrier. Vol. I: Extracts A to D; Vol. II: Extracts E to J. *Further volumes in preparation.*	Demy 8vo	
LETTERS TO THE CHILDREN With 5 plates	Demy 8vo	238 pp.
MINOR PROPHETS	Demy 8vo	250 pp.
PRAYERS AND BLESSINGS	Crown 8vo	64 pp.

SMALLER BOOKS (Paper Bound)

SPIRITUAL HEALING	Demy 8vo	128 pp.
THE MYSTERY OF THE CITY UPON SEVEN HILLS	Demy 8vo	80 pp.
GREAT RECOVERIES	Demy 8vo	80 pp.
THE FESTIVAL OF THE MASS OF ISRAEL	Demy 8vo	72 pp.
THE STORY OF THE SHEPHERDS OF BETHLEHEM	Demy 8vo	72 pp.
THE PATHWAY TO PEACE	Demy 8vo	64 pp.
SUBLIME AFFIRMATIONS	Demy 8vo	64 pp.
WHAT IS A CHRISTIAN?	Demy 8vo	64 pp.
THE SECOND COMING OF CHRIST	Demy 8vo	48 pp.
THE GREAT TRIBULATION. THE WORK	Demy 8vo	44 pp.
THE EVANGEL OF ST. JOHN	Demy 8vo	40 pp.
THE CHRIST FESTIVAL. THE WAYS OF GOD AND THE WAYS OF MEN	Demy 8vo	36 pp.
THE CROSS OF A CHRIST. THE RESURRECTION LIFE	Demy 8vo	36 pp.
THE PASSING OF SOULS	Demy 8vo	32 pp.
THE CONTINUITY OF CONSCIOUSNESS	Demy 8vo	28 pp.
THE SOUL'S JUBILEE	Demy 8vo	28 pp.
IF CHRIST CAME BACK?	Demy 8vo	28 pp.
THE SEASON OF THE CHRIST-MASS	Demy 8vo	24 pp.
A MEDITATION ON GOD	Demy 8vo	24 pp.
THE ORDER OF THE CROSS, WITH CROSS IN COLOUR	Demy 8vo	24 pp.
THE LIFE IMMORTAL	Demy 8vo	20 pp.
THE MESSAGE AND THE WORK	Demy 8vo	16 pp.
THE INNER MEANING OF THE FOOD REFORM MOVEMENT	Demy 8vo	8 pp.
ON BEHALF OF THE CREATURES	Crown 8vo	128 pp.
THOUGHTS FOR THE DAY	Crown 8vo	52 pp.
THE ABRAHAMIC STORY	Crown 8vo	20 pp.

By E. MARY GORDON KEMMIS:

THE "GREATER WORKS" (Cloth bound)	Crown 8vo	64 pp.

FOR USE IN WORSHIP

PSALMS AND CANTICLES FOR WORSHIP	Demy 8vo	96 pp.
HYMNS FOR WORSHIP WITH TUNES	Demy 8vo	280 pp.

All prices on Application